Simpler
Healthcare

Using Lean to Achieve Breakthrough Improvements in Safety, Quality, Access, and Productivity

Marc S. Hafer

Simpler
Healthcare

Using Lean to Achieve Breakthrough Improvements in Safety, Quality, Access, and Productivity

Marc S. Hafer

Dedicated to Gary Krach,

Our colleague,

Our friend,

Our sensei

Acknowledgments

To Simpler® founder Ed Constantine and foundational leaders Doug Goschke and George Koenigsaecker for the opportunity to introduce the Simpler Business System® into healthcare.

To Don Berwick for his encouragement to serve, and to the leaders at ThedaCare, who influenced our approach to healthcare.

To our clients featured in this book who pioneered the use of Lean in healthcare and continue to demonstrate the courage to remain on a never-ending journey of learning:

> Carol Platt, Paul Hetherington, and Triona Buckley of Alder Hey
>
> Phil Goodman of Denver Health
>
> Mary Kingston, Robert Brannigan, David O'Brien, and John Bennett of St. Joseph
>
> Dr. Lim Suet Wun and Professor Philip Choo of Tan Tock Seng
>
> Shirley Appelhans, Joanna Omi, Bill Hicks, Claire Patterson, Todd Hixon, and Joe Alongi of New York City Health and Hospitals Corporation
>
> Ann Schenk and Cindy Walton of Royal Bolton

To our team of sensei who use their decades of experience to mentor and inspire our clients to reach breakthrough improvements in healthcare safety, quality, access, and productivity.

Contents

" *Transformational learning requires deep personal experience.* "

—From the Principles of the Simpler Business System®

Why *Simpler Healthcare?*

Few topics generate as much heat and passion as healthcare reform. Although currently a fixation in the United States because of the national legislation under debate, the topic is highly contested in many countries around the world. As a frequent traveler to England, I have noticed that the national news features stories on the United Kingdom's National Health Service virtually every day. Whether positive or negative, these news stories serve as a daily reminder of the high value individuals place on good health and the great value individuals place on access to high-quality, affordable healthcare. Quite often newscasters describe health systems, healthcare providers, and delivered services with a mixture of love and hate, perhaps even emphasizing the conflicting sentiments to heighten the passion of the dialogue.

Even the most dispassionate healthcare insiders posit that the industry is severely broken on multiple dimensions. At healthcare conference after conference, renowned speakers provide emotional testimonials and expert researchers from the most highly regarded healthcare institutes recite data highlighting the countless performance gaps between "what is" and "what should be" in healthcare. Among healthcare experts there is little debate about what ails healthcare, but the methods of reform and the ideal place to begin generate enormous controversy.

Whether we live in the UK, the US, or any other industrialized nation, as individuals who are also patients, most of us sense that something is grossly wrong with healthcare and that the system is in desperate need of repair. We experience excessive wait times for care; discomfort and sometimes harm from lengthy hospital stays; pain and suffering as the result of hospital-acquired infections and preventable errors; and diminishing expendable income as we pay more for healthcare that appears to have no cost ceiling. As patients, we don't need graphs or statistical validation to form an opinion about the state of healthcare...we *are* the statistics.

At Simpler Consulting, we have witnessed candid self-assessments by administrators, clinicians, and academics in their frenetic searches for the root causes of the problems that afflict the healthcare industry. However, these assessments of safety, quality, access, and costs tend to isolate the specific pathways or service bundles that routinely produce adverse outcomes or the occasional sentinel event. On the basis of these assessments, healthcare administrators and providers tend to focus their attention on failures in specific processes. Senior leaders—who may be only remotely aware of the circumstances that produced the poor outcomes in question—then enact random solutions that fail to address the true systemic or cultural root causes. For this reason, the time-consuming and often costly corrective actions are frustratingly unsustainable.

Simpler was founded on the premise that the Toyota Production System (TPS), commonly known as "Lean management," changes organizational culture, weaving real-time, continuous problem-solving capabilities into the fabric of organizations. The healthcare industry is no exception to this premise; in fact, the logical and scientific methodology rigorously applied in a TPS-like culture easily transfers to healthcare organizations. Furthermore, the tools and techniques employed in a Lean culture help to deconstruct even the most complex health system challenges, enabling staff and leaders to craft basic, logically sound solutions. These solutions are implemented by practitioners at the front lines of care, rather than by improvement/quality experts or administrators, who often are unaware of the clinical implications of proposed changes. When implemented in a culture that enables participation and sets the expectation for engagement in continuous improvement, Lean and TPS not only improve care, efficiency, and value but also build a well-spring of problem-solvers throughout the entire enterprise.

Simpler Healthcare is our initial foray into formally documenting the success of the healthcare industry in deploying Lean and TPS in the culture of their clinical organizations. After more than twenty-five thousand cycles of improvement by Simpler's healthcare clients since 2003, we believe that thousand cycles of improvement by Simpler's healthcare clients, we believe that we have successfully confirmed our hypothesis that when applied consistently and skillfully, Lean can be the potential transformative lever that the healthcare system so desperately needs. We firmly believe that it is time to accelerate the widespread implementation of the Lean approach and achieve true healthcare reform.

Although writing of our clients' experiences runs counter to our belief that humility is an essential element of continuous improvement, we have been moved by the growing interest in Simpler's methods to publicly document the successes of our clients in making continuous process improvement and cultural change a reality.

One of the most admirable characteristics of the members of the healthcare industry is their propensity to collegially share information and solutions without regard to commercial competition. Thus from the point of view of Simpler and similarly devoted practitioners of the Toyota Production System and "Lean" management, we are optimistic and hopeful that success using Lean in healthcare will spread quickly across the globe. We offer our clients' stories in *Simpler Healthcare* as a testimony to the work and determination of the members of these fine organizations to make an enduring contribution to reforming healthcare for all of us.

What You Should Expect

We had many options from which to select the thematic architecture of *Simpler Healthcare,* our first healthcare book. Ultimately we decided that *Simpler Healthcare* would be our "first" rather than our "only" book on transforming healthcare, and thus we set aside many of the intriguing ideas that surfaced regarding *how* to transform healthcare, either healthcare transformation en masse or one value stream at a time. Instead, we engaged a medical writer, with training as a clinician, to interview a handful of leaders and staff from each organization. From these firsthand accounts, the writer collected the lessons learned and insights gleaned from the early years of these organizations' journeys toward Lean transformation.

In these pages, readers will find six vignettes in which healthcare leaders, administrators, and providers apply the Lean approach within their institutions. Each vignette describes the successes and struggles of one of our clients—organizations that pioneered the adoption of Toyota's time-tested methods in an industry that at times seems weary from (and wary of) improvement overload. All six organizations highlighted in *Simpler Healthcare* had experience with Lean, Six Sigma, Total Quality Management, or derivations of these and other "programs." Yet leaders from each were searching for a better way to harness improvement tools and techniques into a systematic methodology—a methodology that could take root, growing beyond temporary solutions to become embedded as a sustainable component of the organization's culture.

In the course of their Lean journeys, leaders and staff of these six healthcare organizations have attained an experiential understanding of core principles, values, and habits of high-performing, Lean organizations. These individuals have seen that when these principles, values, and habits are coupled with the well-documented tools and techniques of Lean, they forge a systematic approach to changing culture. The stories of these individuals show how they experimented with and adapted Simpler's proven systematic change methodology to their local conditions and sought truths to unleash the untapped creativity and enthusiasm for change found in their particular cultures.

We believe that the common elements of Lean management that led to success are not intrinsic characteristics of the healthcare industry ethos; rather, leaders and staff must learn these skills during their early struggles to implement Lean. These common elements for success include:

- Hands-on engagement and involvement of leaders in championing and channeling change behaviors;
- Linkage between Lean transformation to enterprise strategy and converting strategy to action;
- Achievement of breakthrough performance in double-digit percentages year after year; and
- Active involvement of the people who perform the relevant work in defining problems and implementing solutions.

Our client stories are intended to demonstrate typical applications of the Simpler Business System in the early years of Lean transformation. The organizations described in *Simpler Healthcare* vary in their developmental stage along the Transformation Continuum^{SM}, which is a progression from the inception of Lean transformation, characterized by early trials and discovery, through developmental stages that build organizational capabilities and strategic successes using Lean as the enabling force. While these six organizations share many traits and have taken somewhat similar approaches to transformation, we've chosen to focus on the experiences and lessons learned that differentiate these pioneering organizations.

Themes

Alder Hey Children's Foundation Trust: realizing the importance of the leadership habits for successful transformation and developing tools to foster these habits for effectively guiding culture and transformation

Denver Health: demonstrating the effectiveness of un-equivocal CEO involvement and setting stretch improvement targets

Royal Bolton Hospital NHS Foundation Trust: understand-ing the rigor required for effective value-stream improvement, linking strategy to action, and fostering change through em-ployee involvement

New York City Health and Hospitals Corporation: appre-ciating the importance of balancing enterprise strategy with customized hospital-level deployment in a large municipal healthcare system

St. Joseph Health System: personalizing cultural transfor-mation and melding it with performance goals

Tan Tock Seng Hospital: increasing capacity while taking performance improvement to a higher level

Key Take-Aways

If we have been successful with our first public account of healthcare organizations where leaders and staff effectively applied the Simpler Business System to reach their location-specific performance goals, readers will take away the follow-ing concepts:

- Healthcare professionals who are serious about ac-complishing enduring, significant healthcare reform have embraced Lean management principles and be-liefs to accomplish culture change and breakthrough performance.

- Lean management and the Simpler Business System address the critical change dimensions of human de-velopment (safety), quality, service (access) costs, and capacity. Typically, all dimensions improve simul-taneously when they are addressed with an effective approach.

- The dimensions that organizational leaders select to target initially and the tools and techniques they apply are dependent on local conditions. The challenge to leadership is to clearly articulate the vision and reasons for action, guide and adapt a customized Lean deployment methodology on a common platform (e.g., the Simpler Business System), and personally lead the transformation on the front lines.

- True and lasting change requires tremendous courage. Perseverance in overcoming obstacles is an essential component to successful Lean transformation.

We hope that readers will begin to see Lean thinking as a strategic, transformative approach that conscientious professionals can apply to make a difference in their workplace—no matter the location or nature of the work. Like our clients whose courage and success we celebrate in *Simpler Healthcare*, we know from experience that the gap between knowing and believing in Lean concepts is bridged only by doing.

Alder Hey Children's NHS Foundation Trust: Effective Lean Leadership

1

A SNAPSHOT
of Alder Hey Children's NHS Foundation Trust

Located in Liverpool, Alder Hey Children's NHS (National Health Service) Foundation Trust is one of the largest children's hospitals in Europe, serving a catchment area of 7.5 million people and delivering over two hundred and sixty thousand patient episodes of care annually. The three-hundred-and-nine-bed teaching hospital offers twenty pediatric specialty services, as well as community-based and mental health services in more than twenty clinic sites. The organization, which employs about twenty-eight hundred staff members, has designated centers of excellence in the areas of oncology, congenital heart disease, and neurosciences. The organization received Foundation Trust status (greater financial independence) in August 2008.

The X-Factor at Alder Hey

The x-factor is the influence or quality that adds value and drives success.

Look for leadership traits necessary for Lean cultural transformation.

In April 2005, the National Health Service (NHS) of England introduced a new funding system. "Almost overnight, for the first time in our long history, we found ourselves faced with a potential financial deficit. The deficit was a sizable one—about thirty million pounds (about sixty million USD) over three years. We knew we needed to act quickly," reflected Paul Hetherington, director of Performance and Service Improvement at Alder Hey Children's NHS Foundation Trust.

This new funding system of payment by results (PBR) involved payment for individual cases, rather than through block contracts. Executives at Alder Hey point to this singular event as to what drove leadership to embrace Lean as a way to make serious changes in their organization. Staying afloat was the organization's burning platform for performance improvement.

In April 2006, hospital executives created an internal, management-based improvement team charged with bringing about rapid change. They decided to begin immediate deployment of continuous improvement tools. Hetherington reports that the activities were successful in stabilizing the organization financially and keeping its books in the black. However, leadership soon discovered that merely using "tools" would not develop a culture critical to continuous improvement, nor was it sufficient to close the gaps critical to meeting operational targets. One of these targets was referral to treatment time. Failure to achieve this target could inevitably lead to NHS censure, which leads to a range of penalties. After a year, Alder Hey executives realized our approach to improvement was unsustainable. Despite the high energy of the team and some resulting wins, it became obvious that a systemic approach and framework were missing. The approach had been one of a scatter gun, aiming and trying to hit specific problem areas, but not looking at the whole pathway. This meant that although improvement occurred in targeted areas, the rest of the pathway carried on as before. A much more structured, systemic approach was needed—one that engaged the whole organization, not just pockets of it.

Alder Hey executives made a critical decision to engage external assistance and use the Lean methodology to achieve a wide range of goals. They envisioned driving comprehensive change through "RIST" (Rapid Improvement Service Transformation), their name for Lean implementation within the Alder Hey organization. In addition to financial goals, they hoped to improve access to, and quality of, care. The hospital had been struggling to meet critical targets of the NHS, such as referral to treatment times and other access to care indicators, and leaders were keen to remedy the problem. Leadership was also quick to recognize the steady increase of demand for services and was faced with limits of their perceived capacity. Something had to be done quickly to enable future demand to be met. The consequences of not meeting demand would be damaging to the Trust.

A Comprehensive Approach

Alder Hey leadership, with consultant assistance, initiated RIST with an enterprise-wide value-stream analysis (EVSA). Out of this EVSA, an Alder Hey Leadership Team of executives, clinical leaders, and managers identified six value-stream families. Focusing improvement within these families was projected to lead to the elimination of 50 percent of identified waste, with a target savings of approximately £12.5m ($20m):

1. Elective Planned Care
2. Emergency Care
3. Clinical Support Services
4. Governance of the Organization
5. Discharge
6. Community Services

The EVSA provided direction for where to target efforts, with several value streams selected for focused improvement activity. The future state designs for these value streams were planned for implementation in a phased approach during the first year. By the end of the year, all six value-stream families had begun execution of Rapid Improvement Events (RIEs) in order to adequately address the gaps to operational targets fast enough while developing a new culture of rapid change.

3

Leadership Commitment

A key component in creating the desired future state was buy-in from the Leadership Team regarding the feasibility of such a high level of improvement. This achievement was a break-through because healthcare professionals typically demand "evidence" before they will commit to an improvement target.

Early on, the Leadership Team truly understood that in order to develop and implement the desired future state within a complex organization, an internal full-time RIST team would be required. This dedicated team would consist of a program manager, a support administrator, and three RIST facilitators. In addition to this team, nine managers and clinicians were trained, who became local champions. Today this group is responsible for aiding leaders in all aspects of improvement, including event preparation, running rapid improvement events (RIEs), and following through to ensure that improvement gains are sustained.

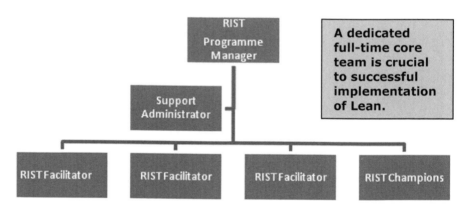

The aggressive pace of change undertaken required the Lean team to execute over seventy RIEs within the course of the first year. The facilitators were trained to run RIEs, help solve problems during event weeks, identify and achieve consensus on the most salient issues, discern potential solutions, and design actions that embodied the Lean principles and techniques. External experts trained, coached, and mentored facilitators to complete these tasks and provided support for more complex and advanced Lean applications.

The work through the six value-stream families took the teams through a variety of pathways, both clinical and non-clinical. Focus remained squarely on the benefits for the Trust in terms of their four vital signs of quality, delivery, cost, and people. The following are just two examples of high-impact areas that were addressed successfully with RIST.

Example of Success: Streamlining Day Case Care

One of the more criti-cal value streams identified during the EVSA was day case surgery and medi-cine. This service line comprised 58 percent of all planned inpa-tient care. "Because we wanted quick wins

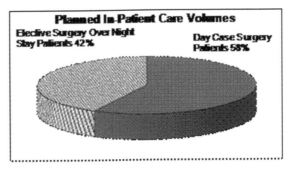

and early wins," says Hetherington, "we decided to look at this very large part of the business." Executives also realized that if the day case unit was able to increase its capacity, some portion of surgical cases currently requiring overnight stays could be handled as day cases, thus releasing beds for other inpatient requirements. Further, addressing capacity limita-tions in both surgical and medical day case throughput could reduce the 20 percent of what was currently true day cases that were ending up as overnight stays and occupying beds on other wards.

Alder Hey execu-tives set a goal of increasing the pro-portion of total cases handled in the day case unit from 58 per-cent to 71 percent, including the target of having no day cases occupy overnight

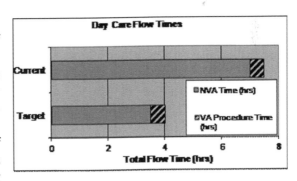

beds. They also set a goal of reducing "flow time," or the time that patients were present on the ward, from an average of 7.5 hours down to 3.5 hours, a reduction of over 50 percent.

Clinical leadership was key to the rapid launch of this pathway. Initially, clinicians were fearful of letting patients down by committing to the increased through-put. However, a leading surgeon and anesthe-tist ran a rapid experi-ment on the Saturday surgical list using the staggered arrival principles and the "bed free" patient plac-es, which resulted in more than a 40 percent improvement in patient throughput.

- Day cases now account for 73 percent of the organisation's surgical procedures.
- Patient Flow time was reduced to under 3.5 hours from 7.5 hours
- Surgical day care capacity increased from 26 to 40 cases per day
- Medical day care capacity increased from 13 to 19 cases per day
- Patient and family satisfaction increased, with a 1/3 reduction in complaints..
- Fewer patients are late for their scheduled start time because of the improved access to the unit.

During a series of rapid improvement events that began in September 2007, the team discovered a flaw in the day case process: patients were "batched," or all scheduled to arrive in the morning, overburdening staff at those particular times. Batching had spillover effects as well, such as parking conges-tion and patient dissatisfaction. During preparation for the first RIE, the team visited the day case ward and observed over ninety-six patients, families, and staff members in the eigh-teen- bed unit. In addition, beds had to be found for day case patients in outlying wards, which created more problems, like long travel times for clinicians. To address the batching prob-lem, the team implemented staggered patient arrival times, which helped reduce the flow time for the patient, reduce the pressure on the inpatient beds, and also relieve the overbur-dening of staff and parking spots.

The team also made changes to the physical layout of the surgical day case area to streamline the flow of patients through the unit. They created a trolley-based system, which freed up space for patients and family members and removed all of the eighteen permanent beds. Based on feedback from patient surveys, the team also created a dedicated parking zone for drop off and pick up nearby, which allowed better access to the day case unit.

The team achieved substantial improvements with the changes they implemented in the day case unit.

With its increased capacity, the unit has been able to accommodate patients who previously would have stayed overnight, thus "converting" overnight cases to day cases. This shift reduced the demand for hospital beds, which was critically important during the winter of 2008, when the hospital, and indeed the whole UK, faced a spike in admissions for respiratory illness. According to Hetherington, "We were able to accommodate those increases for inpatient requirements simply because we had more inpatient beds, freed up from the day-case load. The changes paid off in huge measure." The figures calculated recently showed that, in fact, improvement in day case capacity had freed up around six thousand bed days over a twelve-month time period of which over 50 percent was used to cope with increased unplanned admissions, as well enabling cost reductions through bed closures and summer ward closures. As Carol Platt, RIST Program manager at the hospital, points out, the team achieved this goal without taking up more space or using more staff time. "Although we increased the number of patients going through the units, we didn't have to increase the size of the actual wards, nor did we increase the number of staff on the ward. This translated to a very high productivity increase—approximately 85 percent— basically using existing staff and facilities in a shorter work day and serving more patients."

According to Hetherington, staff on the unit liked the change. "They are more sat-

isfied and the unit is less cluttered and hectic than it was previously. They used to have these horrendous peak times. At eight o'clock in the morning, they would have twenty-six patients at one time. The patients are arriving in a more staggered way now, four or five at a time instead of twenty-six. The staff is finding the new process easier to manage... I think they take greater satisfaction in their work than was previously the case." Platt agrees: "Even though there are more patients going through, staff actually don't feel it—even though they're doing nearly 30 to 50 percent more work than before."

Even after the initial rapid experiment to prove the concept, staff observations included:

"Went smoothly & efficiently with minimal delays."

"Much less troublesome than a normal day!"

"Enjoyed working closely with Clinicians"

"We've been requesting this for years!"

"Patient waiting time was reduced."

Patients and family members also appreciate the streamlined processes in the day case unit. They routinely comment about the efficiency and smoothness of the new process. Executives have received numerous letters from family members, particularly those who visit regularly, commenting on the changes—how much better the quality of the service is now, and how much it has improved the patient/family experience. Comments from patients and family positively surprised the staff, who took the importance of their service for granted:

"How fast it was!"

"It was quick, we didn't wait much."

"After 20 minutes we went to the theatre."

"Very friendly informative staff & a non clinical approach."

"We were basically in & out, and even got to speak to a surgeon."

Example of Success:
Shortening Referral Turnaround Time

Even improvements in non-clinical processes can impact both clinical efficiency and patient experience, as demonstrated through success in simplifying the referral process.

The EVSA highlighted that the outpatient appointment booking process within the clinical services value stream was extremely inefficient and contributed directly to the failure to meet the referral to treatment targets (RTT). Prior to RIST implementation, family members of children who were referred by a general practitioner for specialty care at the hospital waited an average of two weeks before receiving a letter confirming the receipt of this referral. It was only then that they were taken to the next stage of the process and could request to schedule an appointment. This two-week delay resulted in frustration, confusion, and extra phone calls from family members and referring physicians. In addition, the delays were problematic because of the NHS RTT access targets that require the provision of care within eighteen weeks of the request for referral. Also, from a quality perspective, there was the risk of not seeing, diagnosing, and treating the patient as soon as possible. The RIST team ran several RIEs to improve the handling of referral requests. Team members found that the process ran sequentially rather than in parallel. By switching to parallel processing, the team achieved an average turnaround time of twenty-four hours from referral to treatment, compared to the previous average of two weeks. Not only are referrals handled more quickly as a result of RIST changes, but family members and physicians experience less stress and aggravation, as well.

Strategic Moves Ensure Buy-In

Implementation of the desired future state at Alder Hey from the EVSA was also reinforced by adopting a strategic approach to the RIST transformation. Recognizing that the success of Lean implementation depended on an enterprise-wide shift in culture, Alder Hey executives used several strategic tools and techniques to achieve buy-in at all levels of the organization. Leadership saw that successful adoption of the Lean approach required that strategic leaders, management-level leaders, and frontline staff accept responsibility for their respective roles in achieving and sustaining improvement.

The first step was to show that change was needed and that the Lean approach could offer a viable solution. By mapping out how Lean could identify inefficiencies across departments—waste that was previously invisible—the Lean team demonstrated the scope of the existing problem and the possibilities of efficiencies and cost savings with RIST.

Next, the Lean team focused on teaching individuals at all levels of the organization that they had a role to play in RIST. According to Triona Buckley, who was head of organizational development at the hospital at the time, having executives involved in the planning process was essential. "It took quite a long time for everybody to understand that they had a role within improvement, rather than just the person who is the nominated lead for improvement. By developing the policy deployment process, people saw how quality can be affected by improvement, and therefore became much more engaged in the improvement process."

Buckley and commissioned researcher Professor Bill Lucas studied the traits needed for effective leadership of improvement endeavors and engaged the executives in modeling these traits for others. (For more, see end of chapter for "The X Factor at Alder Hey Children's NHS Foundation Trust: Leadership Habits of Mind.") Finally, Lean executives focused on aligning RIST objectives with expectations at the frontlines of care. Buckley found that this alignment was critical for ensuring that change occurred, noting that "the improvement process is quite forward-looking because we're aiming for this future goal, and, as such, it was sometimes regarded as 'It's not my day-to-day business; it's a nice-to-have.' It wasn't until we started to ensure that people were being monitored against what they were doing in moving towards the future breakthroughs, as well as their day-to-day business, that that real shift started to happen."

Averting Resistance of Frontline Staff

Prior to implementing Lean, Alder Hey executives assumed that resistance of frontline staff to a new improvement initiative would be a significant challenge. According to Platt, "We anticipated that people would just see it as another initiative, another flavor of the month." To deal proactively with this potential barrier, executives created an enterprise-wide communications strategy that included grand rounds presentations to physicians, regular staff briefings, routine messages sent via the organization's intranet, and the placement of Lean activities on the agendas of regular meetings within the Trust. Executives also ensured that as many staff members as possible were involved in improvement activities as quickly as possible. Over the first two years, eight hundred attendees—close to one quarter of the hospital's twenty-eight hundred employees—were directly involved in RIEs. In addition, executives assured staff from the inception of the initiative that there would be no layoffs and that any staff redundancies created by increased efficiencies would be addressed through natural attrition. Finally, direct communication about the organization's financial crisis helped overcome staff resistance to change because they knew the alternative might be layoffs.

Engaging Physicians with an Evidence-Based Approach

An initial concern for Hetherington was the question, "How does the Lean approach engage clinicians?" He reflects that the VSA and RIE methodology works very well with clinicians as it has an evidence-based approach, which fits with their own clinical practice of using data and measuring and monitoring indicators to achieve change or care improvement.

Big Picture Results

Alder Hey has achieved improvement that spans the organization. The improvements in productivity realized equate to between fifty and sixty full-time staff members. Honoring the pact made with employees, executives did not reduce staff numbers.

Instead, they expanded services. By improving productivity, the organization now conducts 10 percent more work than before—but without needing to hire additional staff members. This productivity improvement is also evident in the NHS Reference Cost measure, which shows that Alder Hey has reduced their cost index from 131 in 2007 down to 109 in 2009, a 17 percent improvement.

Another substantial improvement the Lean team achieved was reducing average length of stay in the hospital from an average of three days in July 2006 to less than 2.65 days in Oct 2009. Implementing Lean also improved patient satisfaction. According to Hetherington, there have been one-third fewer formal complaints to the hospital than before Lean. "We hoped to reduce complaints and we've exceeded that reduction now. I believe it has a lot to do with Lean."

Looking to the Future

In July 2009, hospital executives engaged in a second EVSA. Participants found that with each pass through the value stream they were able to identify new levels of waste. The original six value-stream families were big, but not focused enough down to individual pathways. According to Hetherington, with the RIST experience acquired in the past two years, the team was able to conduct a more detailed and specific investigation and result in a much clearer identification of needs and targets.

Executives are using information gleaned from this EVSA to help plan the next phase of RIST implementation. Plans include twelve new value streams, each of which is assigned to a process owner responsible for regular reports to the governance board (see explanation below). Alder Hey executives and staff have completed a learning process that places the hospital in good stead for the future. The lessons learned during the first two years of RIST implementation have generated positive energy and commitment from the leadership and all levels of staff.

One opportunity identified was the need for more focused governance of the program, ensuring it was linked to supporting achievement of their long-term goals. These long-term goals have been expressed as the Alder Hey "Vital Signs" (see figure on page 12) and are a simple patient-/family-centric definition of what counts. In fact, the Trust has created a core team of executives, called the Rapid Improvement Transformation Governance Board, charged with direct oversight of RIST implementation across the entire organization. This board ensures that RIST is no longer perceived as an add-on, but is at the core of enabling the delivery of the Trust's strategic objectives.

In Reflection

Executives at Alder Hey Children's NHS Foundation Trust were faced with a daunting challenge when an abrupt shift in NHS funding threatened the financial stability of the entire organization. By engaging leadership to model-specific "habits of mind" that were supportive of improvement and proactively addressing potential staff resistance, the Lean team facilitated effective implementation of the Lean approach and tools throughout the organization. Within an organization that fully embraced Lean, executives and staff were able to steer through a taxing and tricky course to achieve increased efficiency, greater productivity, better patient experience, higher quality of care, and faster delivery of service, all leading to fiscal solvency. The total savings and revenue improvement after just over two years is in excess of £10m ($15m).

The X Factor at Alder Hey Children's NHS Foundation Trust: Leadership Habits of Mind

A key element in the successful implementation of RIST at Alder Hey is the deep appreciation within the organization of the leadership skills required for improvement. While embarking on the Lean journey, Alder Hey executives recognised an opportunity to better understand which leadership characteristics could foster successful organizational transformation. Based on published literature and interviews with staff, the head of organizational development, Triona Buckley, and a commissioned researcher, Professor Bill Lucas, created opportunities for management and executives to engage in leadership approaches thought to be supportive of continuous improvement. This work was enabled through the support of a UK independent charity called The Health Foundation.

By interviewing Alder Hey executives about their improvement work and leadership activities, researchers uncovered four "habits of mind" that exemplified the "Alder Hey way" of leading. These habits included:

1. Being improvement-focused
2. Continuously asking questions about improvement
3. Facilitating the development of improvement capabilities in others, and
4. Empowering others in improvement

According to Buckley, "the management and leadership of the organization then had to role model those habits of mind, or ways of working, and to expect that of others. The fundamental thing we found was that you have to lead in a slightly different way than we were used to in order to maximise the benefits of leading improvement." Through deliberate consideration of the characteristics best suited to maximize improvement and by setting the expectation that management and leadership would model these habits of mind for others, organizational leaders built a cadre of improvement leaders across the organization, which strongly facilitated the successful implementation of RIST.

Denver Health: Rapid Financial Improvements to Maintain Care for All

2

A SNAPSHOT
of Denver Health

Denver Health is an integrated healthcare system that serves approximately one hundred and fifty thousand individuals every year—25 percent of the residents of Denver. In addition to a four-hundred-and-seventy-seven-bed acute care hospital—which houses a regional level 1 trauma center—the academic health system includes a 911 medical response system, a network of family health centers, a regional poison and drug center, school-based health clinics, a health insurance plan, and a correctional care program to provide medical care for incarcerated individuals. Founded one hundred and fifty years ago as the city hospital, the organization remains committed to maintaining access to high-quality care for all. As the state's primary safety net institution, Denver Health serves a population that often struggles with access to care, including individuals who are poor, uninsured, or disenfranchised. In fact, 46 percent of the patients served by the health system are uninsured. The health system also serves as the state's largest Medicare provider.

In 2011, The Shingo Prize for Operational Excellence awarded Denver Health with a Bronze Medallion. This is the first healthcare organization to be honored with a Shingo Prize. The mission of The Shingo Prize is to create excellence in organizations through the application of universally accepted principles of operational excellence, alignment of management systems, and the wise application of improvement techniques across the entire organizational enterprise.

The X-Factor at Denver Health

The x-factor is the influence or quality that adds value and drives success.

Look for the unequivocal CEO involvement to bring about culture change and achievement to stretch goals

Looking to Lean

"Getting It Right: Perfecting the Patient Experience" was formally introduced to the Denver Health family in May, 2004, when Patricia A. Gabow, M.D., chief executive officer and medical

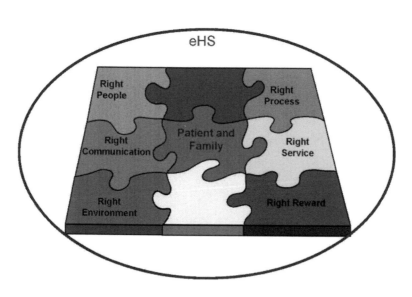

director, delivered her annual State of Denver Health address at the Day of Celebration.

"Denver Health is going to take the road less traveled," she told the standing-room-only crowd that day. "We have only three options when faced with increased uninsured patients and decreased revenues: cut services to the uninsured, increase revenues, or dramatically improve efficiency. We're going to maintain our mission and select the third."

The Lean journey began at Denver Health with the top right-hand corner piece of this puzzle, defined as getting the right process or using Lean tools. Although Denver Health leadership was committed to using Lean principles to make change happen, they soon recognized the need for guidance from Lean experts. This pathway was taken in order to be successful at a pace rapid enough to avoid having to take drastic financial measures. Denver Health has been on this path since April 2005.

Because of the urgent need to eliminate waste in the system and reinvest funds into clinical care, Denver Health leaders aggressively chose to launch five initial value streams. These value streams offered the greatest opportunity for improvement in efficiency based on their True North metrics:

1. Patient access
2. Operating room
3. Billing (revenue cycle)
4. Outpatient clinic flow
5. Inpatient hospital flow

Over the years, Denver Health has learned that to truly improve healthcare, focus needs to be placed in both clinical and non-clinical areas of their organization, which is reflected in the balance of value streams chosen.

True North Metrics

Focus equally on all five:

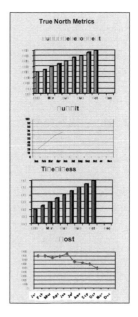

1. Human Development
   - Improved capability at all levels
2. Quality
   - Zero defects
3. Timeliness (Service and Access)
   - 1 by 1, in sequence, on demand
4. Cost
   - 100% value added
5. Growth/Capacity
   - Care for more people

Creating Organizational Capacity

In launching the efforts of Lean, three key individuals were assigned to each value stream: an executive sponsor, responsible for monitoring overall outcomes, a value-stream owner, responsible for all aspects of the particular value stream effort, and a process owner, responsible for individual RIEs in an assigned area. As outlined in the Denver Health Transformation Plan of Care (TPOC^SM), these value-stream leaders, in close coordination with their assigned facilitator from the Lean Systems Improvement Team, were responsible for ensuring that a minimum number of RIEs were completed within their value stream during the twelve-month period following the value-stream analysis. In addition to event coordination, the value-stream trio also conducted monthly Value-Stream Steering Committee meetings, following strict standard work to ensure proper event selection, preparation, execution, and sustainment. Each facilitator was assigned two value streams, with the expectation that eight RIEs would be completed per value stream.

These requirements ensured that enough time was dedicated to achieve successful change and allowed the organization to maintain a steady rhythm of activities. It also allowed the organization to build on its momentum and synergies and to ensure that required change was not needlessly delayed.

An Early Win

According to the organization's senior Lean facilitator, Philip Goodman, Denver Health leaders selected initial RIEs that were likely to achieve early, quick, and significant victories and thus gain organizational buy-in. Beginning with the very first value stream and RIE, the health system realized significant cost savings and waste reduction across all of its selected value streams.

The initial RIE in the operating room value stream was especially effective in gaining momentum for the organization because of its rapid positive results. Held in June 2005, the first RIE focused on antibiotic administration in the operating room (OR) of the health system's acute care hospital. Prior to the intervention, OR staff managed to achieve the requirement of prophylactic antibiotic administration within sixty minutes of incision for approximately three-quarters of procedures. The current state process in which antibiotics were administered on the floor or pre-op holding area "on call to OR" often resulted in missing the sixty-minute window due to delays, rescheduled procedures, or inefficient room turnover.

In the initial week-long RIE, staff developed an improved future state process. Along with other improvements, the order sheet was changed so that anesthesia staff administered antibiotics once the patient arrived in the OR rather than before. By the next week, approximately 96 percent of patients requiring prophylactic antibiotics received them within the recommended timeframe (see figures). According to the chief of anesthesiology, John Lockrem, M.D., the RIE "changed our practice in just three days." The statement is doubly impressive given that the hospital's anesthesiology practice had a long history of being independent and autonomous in setting their practice standards.

Surgical Site RIE Case Study

DENVER HEALTH
Level One Care for ALL

1.Reason for Action SCIP II requires abx within 60 minutes of "first cut"	**2. Initial Condition** Prophylactic abx in OR within 60 mins < 80% of cases	**3.Target Condition** Prophylactic abx in OR within 60 mins in 100% of cases
4.Gap Analysis Abx given "OCTOR" Variable abx APC Frustration OR Frustration	**5.Solution Approach** Conduct waste walk Map process RIE to include IC Chart review	**6.Rapid Experiment** Change OCTOR to "Abx delivered in OR by anesthesiologist" Abx guidelines
7.Completion Plans Change order forms Monitor data	**8.Confirmed State** Per Dr Lockrem: "We've changed our practice"	**9.Insights** The problem was definitely the process, not the people!

Clinical RIE Case Study Results

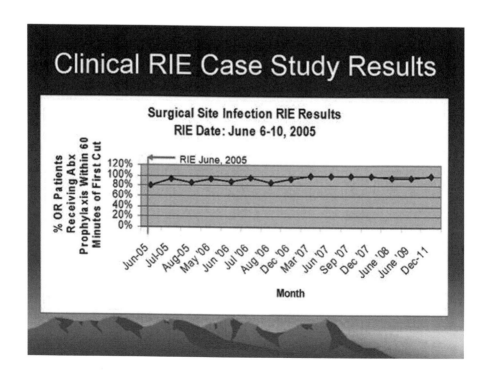

Surgical Site Infection RIE Results
RIE Date: June 6-10, 2005

Due in part to a highly engaged nursing OR director, who follows OR metrics closely, these patient safety practices have been sustained since implemented four years ago. When the compliance percentage dipped in one quarter, she uncovered the root cause: outdated order forms had slipped back into the OR administrative offices. With a simple fix, the numbers soared again and have remained close to 100 percent since that time. It confirmed the understanding that sustainment does not just happen; it must be earned through close monitoring and hard work.

This early victory paved the way for additional RIEs across the health system, including those focused on cost savings rather than strictly on clinical care. The victory also served as a boost to staff engagement in Lean. According to Goodman, the early wins were critical for engaging and aligning staff with the Lean approach. "Over time, after a series of RIEs, the staff began to cooperate with each other's events with the sense that 'We'll help implement the changes for their team's RIE this month, and they'll support our changes next month.'" To date, more than fifteen hundred employees have actively participated in more than three hundred and twenty-five RIEs, representing more than 25 percent involvement rate of total employees.

Lean Contributes to Significant Cost Reductions

Despite a focus on increasing efficiency, the organization's economic climate progressively worsened during the period from 2005 to 2008. In 2007, Denver Health provided two hundred and seventy-six million dollars in care for uninsured patients, only a portion of which was reimbursed by city, state, and federal agencies. By 2008, the cost of care for uninsured patients reached three hundred and eighteen million dollars, but because of governmental budget reductions, the reimbursement dollars did not keep pace. Further, due to job loss in the recession, financial experts were not surprised when uninsured care in 2009 reached three hundred and sixty-two million dollars. The 2010 numbers show yet an additional rise to three hundred and eighty-eight million dollars (see insert).

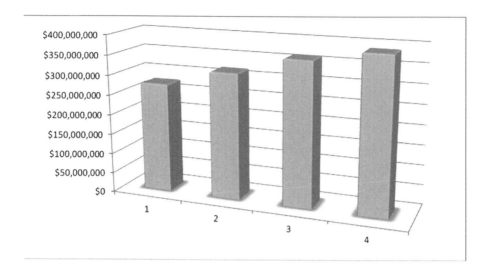

As these numbers have grown, Denver Health leaders have had choices: cut specific health programs, reduce patient services, cut staff hours, or find a way to wring additional waste from the system. Dr. Gabow and her executive team chose the last, not only committing fully to Lean implementation, but searching for ways to accelerate the pace of Lean transformation. When many organizational leaders would have pulled back the reins and reduced activities, Denver Health leaders pushed forward an aggressive Lean journey by consistently increasing levels of Lean activities: the pace of event weeks, the number of events, and the number of people involved.

Accelerating Lean: Denver Health Black Belts

As another means for accelerating Lean transformation, Denver Health leaders expanded the organization's in-house and completely unique Lean Black Belt program. In contrast to the more traditional, purely statistically based Six Sigma Black Belt approach, the Denver Health program more appropriately defined its program as Lean Black Belts. The prospective Lean Black Belts receive training that includes a broad base of Lean tools and techniques. This training allows for a more widespread application of the improvement process than is possible by simple attendance on an RIE team or with other Black Belt programs. Initiated by Dr. Gabow in the fall of 2004, the program provides intensive training in techniques and tools to selected Denver Health staff. Candidates, whose participation must be recommended by Denver Health leaders and approved by Dr. Gabow, include physician directors, nursing directors, service line administrators, and mid-level managers. Appointment to a Black Belt position is uncompensated but considered an honor within the institution. With fifty participants at initiation, the program has since expanded to one hundred and ninety-six certified Lean Black Belts, with plans to further expand training efforts by fifty per year until four hundred Black Belts are in place at the organization. In 2009, thirty-six Black Belts took advanced training to become Master Black Belts.

After completing intensive training, Black Belts are charged with working in parallel with the centralized Lean Systems Improvement department, the senior Lean facilitator, and the external Sensei on individual cost-saving projects. Value Stream Executive Sponsors have the option of utilizing the Lean Black Belts within their value stream for RIE project completion. This optional use of the Lean Black Belts has allowed for tremendous acceleration of completion plans. Black Belts are required to submit a Black Belt project report every other month that details progress in their goal of achieving thirty thousand dollars in savings over twelve months. The savings are verified by the finance department during weekly meetings with the deputy CFO and appropriate budget analysts. Guidelines for verification of savings are exceptionally strict to ensure that the Black Belt program results in an immediate and traceable path to the financial bottom line of the organization.

Putting Lean principles to work among individuals working at the frontlines of care has proven a very successful means for rapidly spreading the Denver Health Lean Transformation throughout the organization. These Black Belt projects are now fully integrated with the value-stream improvement activities. To date, more than five hundred Lean Black Belt projects have been submitted, with confirmed savings of twenty-one million dollars and countless non-monetary improvements. This is an impressive return on investment.

Wins across the System

Cost-efficiency projects at Denver Health have ranged from simple to complex. For example, a Black Belt who worked in the correctional area of the hospital noticed that virtually all of the incarcerated patients' box lunches were returned with the fruit portion uneaten. The fruit was tossed with the rest of the refuse. Subsequently, fruit was removed as a standard item in the lunches—and the health system netted thirty-two thousand dollars in savings annually with no negative impact on patient satisfaction. This example of waste reduction—and many others across the health system—is dependent on the attentiveness of clinical staff that are trained in the Lean approach of being able to first identify then being able to eliminate the wastes that they find in their everyday work life. The combination of their knowledge of Lean tools and clinical applications has been essential to rooting out inefficiencies and realizing true cost savings.

An example that involved a more complicated calculation of cost savings and efficiencies was the placement of pharmacists within primary care offices to improve clinician efficiency. Initial investigation showed that pharmacist review of patients' records prior to visits was ineffective at improving the efficiency of primary care physicians. However, physically locating pharmacists within the practice setting proved very effective. The health system achieved cost savings that not only covered the salary of the pharmacist but also netted thirty thousand dollars per pharmacist. System leaders anticipate that the presence of pharmacists additionally will improve medication reconciliation, allow clinicians to spend more time in direct care, increase the use of generic medications, and foster clinician education.

In addition to contributing to direct savings, Black Belts continue to have a major impact on the process improvement portion of the Denver Health Lean Enterprise Transformation as well. One value stream that has reaped large financial rewards across the system is the revenue cycle value stream. Many Black Belt projects have been focused on the charge capture portion of this value stream. Black Belts have assessed charges in various departments and have identified many services and goods for which charges were not being properly recorded. By alerting relevant staff members to the need for changes in the standard work, Black Belts "found" new revenue for Denver Health.

Cost Savings Exceed Predictions

Through proactive application of the combined "one-two punch" of Lean Black Belts and value-stream approach, Denver Health leaders and staff achieved cost savings that were greater than originally expected. As recently as January 2009, the goal of Denver Health CEO was to achieve savings of $5.5 million during the 2009 calendar year. With the rapid expansion of focused Lean techniques, including the inclusion of the full-time Sensei model, these goals had to be drastically revised. For 2009, the verified savings/cost avoidance to Denver Health was twenty million dollars, which is double the combined amount of savings from the prior four years. The 2010 numbers have just been verified and are even more astounding. Savings in 2010 more than doubled again to over forty million dollars for the year (see figure). Black Belt savings were $8.5 million for the 2010 year and one value stream, revenue cycle, yielded ten million in savings!

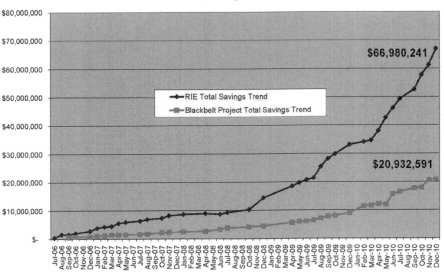

RIE + Blackbelt Financial Benefit Trend
Cumulative Through December 31, 2010

The Secrets of Success

Many factors led to the success of Denver Health in recapturing waste within the system and cutting costs, while continuing to provide high-quality care. The cumulative experience of four years of working with the Lean approach and tools allowed the organization to build on a foundation of skills and knowledge to rapidly accelerate progress in the fifth year of the endeavor. The decision of Denver Health leaders to further expand this Lean initiative with the full-time Sensei concept and increased Denver Health resources, in the face of a worsening economic climate, has proven to be a wise choice. It demonstrates that the Lean journey requires time, investment, and commitment to build enough organizational capacity and critical mass to reach the "tipping point" that results in accelerated returns from Lean processes and improvements.

In retrospect, Philip Goodman, senior Lean facilitator, believes that early victories and direct involvement in change initiatives were critical to staff engagement and alignment. His perception is supported by survey data showing that participation in an RIE is the factor most closely associated with high levels of Denver Health staff engagement. Dr. Gabow's attention to staff engagement, and direct involvement of a full-time Sensei, were also critical to the organization's success.

Looking to the Future

Denver Health leaders have a number of plans for continuing expansion of Lean within the health system. They plan to train an additional two hundred and fifty Black Belts by the end of 2014, for a total of four hundred. In November 2009, the organization launched an extremely successful Master Black Belt graduate training program, which will add classes each year. This will expand the capacity of the health system to implement Lean at an even higher level of velocity and expertise. Health system leaders have set an additional major goal: the reallocation of one hundred thousand square feet of physical space. Achieving this objective will save Denver Health millions of dollars in remodeling and construction costs as demand for service expands.

The Denver Health integrated system has been established as an ideal model of healthcare delivery, one that serves as an example in healthcare reform debates at the national level. The Lean initiative has made the organization's story even more compelling, demonstrating that millions of dollars of healthcare costs can be eliminated through the application of process improvement principles like Lean. Thus, a simple goal—to survive the financial crises—has led to creation of a mature culture that is committed to reducing waste in order to achieve a perfect patient experience, and continues to serve as a model for the nation.

The Journey So Far

When faced with a dim financial picture, Denver Health leadership chose to continue supporting the organization's central mission of quality care for all and embark on the journey to Lean transformation. Despite a worsening economic climate, organizational leaders fully embraced a Lean approach and techniques, expanding rather than contracting them when the economy weakened. By focusing on staff and leadership engagement, achieving an early win, and persisting with Lean transformation over the course of several years, the organization has successfully upheld its central mission—providing the highest quality of care to all, regardless of ability to pay—while serving as a national model for the efficient delivery of high-quality care.

Denver Health appears poised to become a health system that politicians and clinicians alike would want to replicate.

The X Factor at Denver Health: A Dedicated Leader with Vision

Thirty-seven years ago, nephrologist Dr. Patricia Gabow joined Denver Health as chief of the renal division. In the early 1980s, she was promoted to director of the medical service for the organization. She became chief executive officer for Denver Health in 1992. Gabow has been named as one of the top twenty-five women in healthcare, one of the top fifty physician executives, and one of the hundred most powerful people in American healthcare.

Gabow's passion for improvement stems from her commitment to expanding access to quality care for those who might otherwise go without. As she tells new staff at the weekly new employee orientation, "The beauty of coming to work at Denver Health is that you can leave work every day and feel you've done something good for people and for the health of this community."

Gabow's strong vision and close involvement with staff have been critical to the organization's success with Lean. From inception, Gabow set clear-cut expectations for full engagement at the executive level in Lean initiatives. Gabow personally monitors the executives' performance in guiding and sustaining increased efficiency for their assigned value streams. In monthly reviews with Lean facilitators, if an RIE isn't meeting the projected metrics, Gabow will personally query the executive sponsor about the project via email immediately after the meeting. She leads by example and routinely participates in *gemba* walks. Gabow works diligently to keep the organizational mission at the forefront of employees' minds, reminding frontline clinicians that any cost savings achieved are a means to expand care for patients. She also ensures that staff, managers, and organizational leaders are carefully selected for their commitment to the Denver Health mission of quality care for all. Following her lead, Denver Health employees—whether clinicians, managers, executives, or non-clinical staff—are aligned around this common mission. Gabow's vision and her focus on alignment and engagement of staff have been crucial factors in the organization's success.

Denver Health is an exceptionally mission-focused organization, strongly committed to providing access to the "highest quality healthcare, whether for prevention or acute and chronic diseases regardless of ability to pay." Through frequent articulation of their mission and deliberate hiring practices, the CEO of the health system, Patricia Gabow, M.D., has worked to embed this commitment to quality care for all into the organizational culture. When faced several years ago with reduced reimbursement and an increasing pool of uninsured patients, the Denver Health leader looked for strategic solutions other than reducing access and services. Six years ago, Gabow discovered Lean and launched the Denver Health journey to Lean transformation.

Royal Bolton Hospital: Increasing Efficiency, Saving Lives

3

A SNAPSHOT
of Royal Bolton Hospital

Royal Bolton Hospital, located in the town of Bolton in Northwest England, became a National Health Service Foundation Trust Hospital (Foundation Trusts enjoy a greater degree of financial freedom within the English National Health Service) in October 2008. The organization serves Bolton (population: two hundred and sixty-five thousand) and some other parts of the Greater Manchester area, providing comprehensive acute care and mental health services. The hospital maintains a staff of thirty-six hundred for its six hundred and seventy-one inpatient beds, thirty-two day-case beds, and fifteen endoscopy beds. An additional four hundred and ten individuals will be hired in the near future as the hospital expands care for a regional initiative called Making It Better, which has designated Royal Bolton Hospital to be one of three centers for excellence for maternity, neonatal, and pediatric care in the metropolitan area of Greater Manchester. The Trust is now one of the early adopters of end to end healthcare and has taken over the community healthcare service provision for Bolton increasing staff to over 7,000 posts and are using Lean principles to create an end to end health system.

The X-Factor at Royal Bolton

The x-factor is the influence or quality that adds value and drives success.

Looking for the balance between tools and culture in a Lean enterprise

The year 2004 was a challenging one for leaders at Royal Bolton Hospital. A new CEO was at the helm and the organization was struggling to cap a spiraling financial deficit as the UK Treasury projected cutbacks in allocations to the English National Health Service (NHS) through changes in the government funding mechanism. There were significant problems with waiting times for treatments and services at the hospital and mortality figures exceeded those of comparable hospitals. The Royal Bolton executives realized that the hospital could not respond effectively to these challenges without a new approach.

Early Experiments with Continuous Improvement

As part of the Institute for Healthcare Improvement's (IHI) 100,000 Lives Campaign, hospital staff and leaders learned about the Lean approach from a Simpler Healthcare[SM] sensei, who was assigned as part of the campaign to work with hospital staff for three months. The Royal Bolton executives were familiar with Lean from previous activities, and this hands-on experience with the tools and techniques during the campaign convinced them to investigate the approach in more depth as a solution to their financial and quality-related issues. In doing so, Royal Bolton Hospital became one of the first NHS Trust hospitals to apply the Lean approach and tools and reap the rewards of rapidly achieved waste reduction and quality improvement.

Getting Started and Setting the Stage

In October 2006, Royal Bolton Hospital decided to engage external assistance to help them accelerate their Lean journey, and staff and leaders were guided to conduct an enterprise-wide value-stream analysis (EVSA), personally led by the CEO, David Fillingham. The EVSA identified major wastes and improvement opportunities in the hospital. During the event, participants identified acute stroke care as one key area for improvement and as the initial value stream to be developed. There was ample room for improvement! The standardized mortality rate for stroke at the hospital was higher than the national average

and the length of stay much longer than ideal. The group also selected the four True North goals for the organization by adding human development (people) to the previously established Trust goals, based on the Triple Aim set by the Institute for Healthcare Improvement. The objectives of the selected True North goals are to improve health, deliver value for money, provide the best possible care, and take joy and pride in work. David and the team developed the above graphic to represent the True North goals—an image that has since adorned countless Bolton presentations.

Developing Organizational Capability

The hospital service improvement team led by Director of Service Improvement Ann Schenk, worked over a period of three years with Simpler to create the Bolton Improving Care System (BICS), which is an adaptation of the Lean approach and terminology, customized for both the Bolton and the NHS culture. This shift in language helped avoid the potential confusion and alienation that sometimes accompanies implementation of a new system with unfamiliar jargon. This diagram shows the current set-up of the organization, established to support implementation of BICS. The BICS associates (staff members trained in Lean) and the assistant facilitators have been added since the team was established in 2006, representing continuing investment in the program.

While hospital leaders were committed to driving improvement across all four of their True North metrics, they also believed that the BICS approach would actually save patient lives.

Applying Lean to Save Lives— Redesigning Stroke Care

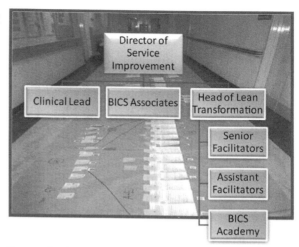

In January 2007, just three months after completing the enterprise-wide VSA, the BICS team conducted the hospital's first pathway

One of the current state maps representing breakdown in the patient flow within the stroke pathway.

value-stream analysis (VSA) for stroke care. A multidisciplinary team, including the consultant lead for stroke, hospital support staff, a health commissioner, and representatives from primary, community, and social care, undertook a week-long value-stream analysis event that reviewed the current state stroke end-to-end patient pathway. The team documented many examples of waste found in hospital processes. For example, patients traveled as far as 4.5 miles around the hospital before arriving at their assigned care unit, with as many as three hundred and ninety-six hand-offs of information during the admission process, neither of which added value to the patient experience (see hand-off diagram in adjacent figure).

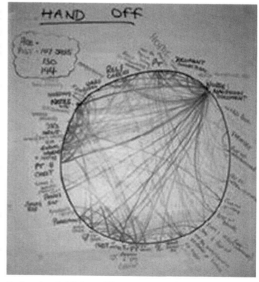

A typical Value-Stream Analysis hand-off diagram representing information flows within the stroke pathway.

At that time, there was no dedicated unit for acute stroke care in the hospital and patients with acute stroke were treated in many different acute care wards located throughout the hospital. In fact, just thirteen dedicated rehabilitation beds off the main spine of the hospital were shared with other acute services.

As they went through this process, team members differentiated the steps that added value to the patient from those that were wasteful, non-value-added steps, which frequently included waiting and duplication. This information was used to create the current state map, as demonstrated in the photograph below. The BICS methodology uses this highly visual form of mapping, as opposed to computer-generated process maps, so that all team members and guests can see the whole process and, therefore, the waste. The team also determined takt times, or patient throughput rates, with an objective to more closely understand the mismatch between discharge rates and admission demand.

The Future State—What Could Good Look Like?

Lean principles were then used to create a future state value-stream map. The future state was designed to reduce the number of hand-offs, remove wasteful delays and duplications from the system, and improve communication among all parties involved in the process, including patients, relatives, and community and social care providers, as well as hospital staff.

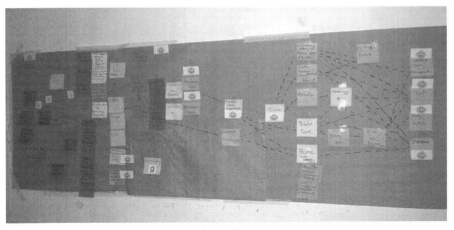

The Future State Map for the stroke pathway.

The future state vision included goals of reducing the number of steps from one hundred and seventy to eighty, decreasing the number of information hand-offs from three hundred and ninety-six to one hundred and twenty-nine, and drastically reducing the average length of stay by 45 percent while avoiding additional readmissions. A highly detailed action plan was developed to guide the acute-care stroke Lean initiative implementation. At the end of this week-long VSA, the team presented the vision for the improved pathway, the action plan, and the projected benefits to the hospital and primary care executives and staff.

Implementation through Rapid Improvement

Over the next few months, the BICS team ran rapid improvement events (RIEs) to implement this future state. The RIE focused on developing standard work for all disciplines involved in the patient pathway, improving goal-setting by implementing use of a goal-attainment scale, and redesigning the information boards to improve communication among members of the multidisciplinary care team.

At this point, it became clear that significant improvement in acute stroke care was contingent on the creation of a specialized unit with appropriately trained staff. The team used the BICS process development tool, a 2P, for planning and designing new processes to develop a new care pathway in detail. The 2P is a standardized Lean tool that helps teams focus on the needs of the patient first, by considering the key steps as the patient progresses through the care pathway. The team developed plans for establishing an entirely new acute-care stroke unit in an existing ward and upgrading the existing stroke rehabilitation unit by relocating it to a new area. The team then used the "asset" tool to model the correct number of beds required using national demographic guidelines. The 2P process also helped to identify the equipment required for both the new acute stroke unit and the rehab unit.

Cindy Walton, the BICS facilitator for the pathway, commented later that "the 2P was an absolute lynchpin during the development of the pathway converting the VSA Future State Vision into action." During this detailed design phase, the team met with the CEO and director of nursing and performance to gain commitment that an adequate location was available, and were surprised when they found that a suitable unit would be available for occupation within six months of the VSA. The rapid approach of BICS accelerated the analysis and approval process, which would have taken years using former project methodologies.

In order to plan the layout for the new acute-care unit, team members created a list of the equipment and furniture the unit would need, and then visited various other units in the hospital, including the cardiac, acute assessment, and high-dependency units to learn more about the set-up of specialist care wards. The team then sketched various layouts, and staff evaluated the designs based on the BICS attribute criteria. The architect for the project was present during this 2P event (Process Preparation—Lean design) to immediately answer questions about the feasibility of any proposed changes. The outcome of this design event was a detailed layout, a comprehensive catalogue of the equipment needed, and a robust timing plan for implementation of the unit. The BICS process demonstrated that a "new unit" could be developed without the need for significant investment in facilities and equipment. The BICS team called this a "paper doll" or cardboard engineering, and found it to be a more realistic design tool than a computer based model, and required less technical input.

A similar approach was taken for designing the existing stroke rehabilitation unit. The Lean team catalogued the equipment they would need for the new rehabilitation unit, with an essentials list and a wish list. They visited the site of the proposed new unit, as well as the existing unit, and inventoried the furniture and equipment, earmarking and tagging those items that could be moved to the new unit.

The team also used the BICS 6S tools in the current stroke rehabilitation unit, which resulted in clearing out the store rooms of seldom-used items, cleaning both the room and the equipment to reduce the risk of infection, and creating a well-organized workplace in which equipment and supplies needed could be found without delay. Over several RIEs, the team condensed two store rooms into one, removed defective and obsolete stock, and implemented a straightforward, uncomplicated visual management system in the stock room using clear labeling and color coding.

Additionally, the 6S process gave a clear understanding of consumption rates for supplies, which enabled the more effective use of existing inventory systems. The staff was also trained to order supplies online, which reduced the supply-replenishment time to one day or less and significantly reduced the number of supply queries, which often delay the prompt payment of suppliers' invoices. Using this online system also reduces the amount of paperwork and the need for physical files, thus freeing up additional space and staff time. To ensure sustainment, the team developed and introduced a daily task control board, on which the shift leader was able to give the staff an accurate picture of the status of work in the rehabilitation unit at a single glance. The board allowed the care team to rapidly assess patient status at shift turnovers and during shifts. By moving the shift handover from back offices to the ward and shortening the time for the nurses' report, staff consequently had more time for direct patient care. The twenty-bed acute-care stroke unit was opened in July 2007, less than six months after the VSA.

Stock Room **Before**

Stock Room **After**

Continuous Improvement

The fifth BICS principle is perfection (principles one to four are customer, value stream, flow, and pull). To ensure continued improvements, the BICS team held RIEs to enhance the newly opened acute unit and to continue planning for the opening of the rehabilitation unit over the following months. Team members held 6S events in the unit to further improve the layout and processes and a continuous 6S audit program ensured that ongoing efficiency was maintained and improved. On a second pass, the team reviewed the physical layout of the unit and was able to further reduce the distance traveled by staff by more than 60 percent per day. Simple and inexpensive improvements, such as the introduction of point-of-use supplies in the hyper-acute bays and the purchase of a phone, significantly reduced motion and wasted time. Overall, the introduction of the new layout, work processes, and visual management has freed up substantial staff time, which has been redirected toward activities that truly add value to patients with stroke, including diagnosis, treatment, and rehabilitation. This series of discrete, small improvements, linked with visionary work to redesign the processes of care, led to improved efficiency, resulting in reductions to length of stay, improved patient care, and lower mortality figures.

BICS was not just about efficiency, but was also designed to improve patient and visitor satisfaction. The BICS team ran a further RIE to make all areas of the new unit more patient-friendly. A stroke information board located on the corridor of the acute unit offers real-time data against the national indicators of care, enabling real-time assessment against the sentinel audit key indicators.

The Bolton stroke unit is an excellent example of continuous improvement in healthcare, where multiple passes create even further improvement after the first RIE. The changes made in process, workflow, and organization ultimately resulted in a substantial impact where it matters most: saving patients' lives.

Quality, Mortality, and Efficiency Improve

The Royal College of Physicians Sentinel Audits monitor the capability and performance within stroke units in all hospitals across the UK every two years. The results from 2008 audit highlighted the significant improvements in acute stroke care and waste reduction that the BICS and stroke team achieved (see chart). In accordance with practice guidelines, 100 percent of patients with acute stroke now have a CT scan performed within twenty-four hours of first contact and 100 percent receive anti-platelet treatment within twenty-four hours of first contact, if appropriate to their condition. In addition, 99 percent of acute stroke patients are admitted to the stroke unit and spend more than 50 percent of their stay under specialized stroke care. Consequently, the average length of stay has dropped from forty-three days to twenty-three days. Finally, the mortality rate for patients with acute stroke has dropped from 122 to 99 (see table). The hospital's overall audit score in 2008 was the fifth highest in the UK. The figure above demonstrates the improvement achieved in these key outcomes.

Not only has patient care improved with the Lean approach and tools, but staff satisfaction has benefitted as well. According to a physiotherapist working on

Sentinel Audit	2006	2008
% patients with CT Scan within 24 hours	44%	100%
% patients receiving therapy within 72 hours	64%	100%
Complex In-patient Length of Stay days	29	<20
Standardised Mortality Rate (100 = national ave.)	122	100
Overall Sentinel Audit Score	60%	92%

Stroke Unit Performance Improvement 2006-8

the unit, "I like BICS because it helps us structure tasks into manageable pieces, which can be worked on systematically." Stroke Unit matron Suzanne Lomas concurs, "We strive for the best possible care for our patients. Using BICS methodology, we are getting there. The outcomes are reflected in improved job satisfaction, patient satisfaction scores, and feedback from the National Sentinel Audits." Patients with acute stroke also appreciate the changes at Royal Bolton Hospital. A patient interviewed as part of the "voice of the customer" research in April 2009 said, "I can't fault anything. It's a very frightening time when you can't walk, or even stand or sit up, but I'm slowly getting mobile and looking forward to going home." With the positive patient feedback and other

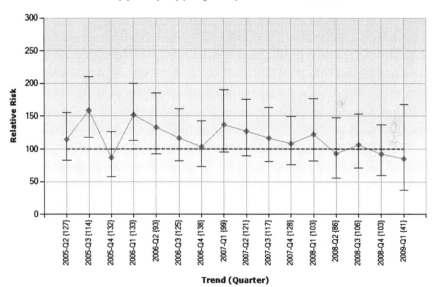

Stroke Unit relative risk reduction trend 2005-9

workplace changes, staff morale has improved. One of the strongest indicators of staff satisfaction is the reduction in average sick leave. Within the new stroke unit, the absence rate has declined from an annualized rate of 15 percent to just 3.5 percent.

Using the BICS process to create the new acute-stroke unit has supported the financial bottom line of the Trust, as well. To build an entirely new unit and hire new staff would have involved significant capital expenses and in-creased labor costs. Applying the BICS approach to create a new unit with existing space and equipment avoided this expense.

Hurdling the Barriers

When the new acute-stroke care unit opened several months earlier than anticipated, the team was faced with pulling to-gether staff that were not yet trained in stroke care tech-niques. The new care team was taken from other areas in the hospital and had to bond as a team and learn new skills fairly quickly. All staff members had volunteered to be on the staff in the new unit, so enthusiasm was high, but many staff members hadn't dealt directly with acute stroke patients before. The hospital leaders ensured that staff had sufficient time for on-the-job training to acquire the necessary skills and set up a teaching program in which staff new to the unit was "buddied" with colleagues already experienced in stroke care.

The greatest challenge to the new unit, however, has not been staff training. The biggest challenge was establishing a reputation for the acute care team and an awareness of the unit among healthcare colleagues within the hospital and through-out the local health system to ensure that patients present-ing with stroke-like symptoms were immediately sign-posted to the unit without delay. The team has held educational ses-sions to raise awareness and presented the evidence-base sup-porting the benefits of specialised care for patients with acute stroke. Leadership commitment within the unit was critical to the successful development of the unit. Gillian Halstead, lead consultant, and Suzanne Lomax, matron on the acute stroke unit, encouraged staff to apply the BICS approach and tools consistently. Their visible engagement in the process supported continuous improvement and the sustaining of achieved gains within the unit.

Applying BICS across the Hospital

The BICS approach has been rigorously applied throughout the hospital. To date, over two thousand members of the staff—more than 75 percent of staff at Royal Bolton—have participated directly in at least one of the over three hundred, week-long RIEs conducted. More than 80 percent of staff has received basic Lean training. Success has not been restricted to just the stroke unit. At the time of writing, the Trust has completed redesign of fourteen patient pathways and sixteen supporting or enabling services. Typical examples of success include:

Suzanne Lomax, matron and recipient of an award for leadership in the application of improved patient care

- Model pathways: the BICS team developed a model for pathways that has significantly reduced LoS and mortality and increased patient throughput via the introduction of a "patient gateway" concept that delivers the right care, at the right time and the right place.
- Trauma care: 50 percent reduction in mortality for patients with hip fracture and a 33 percent reduction in length of stay
- Orthopedics: 85 percent reduction in complications associated with high-risk joint replacement surgery and 43 percent reduction in length of stay; and
- Non-clinical value streams (laundry, finance, and physical plant) and clinical support services (pharmacy, blood sciences, and health records departments) contributed cost savings in the seven-figure range.

Looking to the Future

The early results in the stroke care and other value streams inspired hospital leaders to stretch their goals in stroke care and expand BICS to additional value streams. To achieve these goals and improvements in other value streams, the hospital leadership developed the "BICS Academy," internal training in BICS skills to support the in-house BICS team. In addition, hospital leaders have begun to train members of the BICS team to become internal change consultants and prepare another one hundred staff members over the next year to run RIEs under the supervision of the new internal BICS change consultants.

The stroke unit continues to strive to meet the challenging new standards established by the national guidelines and regional programs such as Advancing Quality.

The hospital has also been recognized as a center of excellence for maternity, neonatal, and pediatric services in the Greater Manchester region, requiring the BICS team to redesign end-to-end patient flow through the design of a new facility and processes. Using the BICS 2P process, the final design is being completed at many millions of pounds below the original estimate.

Reflection

Royal Bolton Hospital leaders embraced Lean transformation as a means for dealing with a spiraling financial deficit, failure to meet national performance targets, and to begin an irreversible culture change. Committing resources and leadership to the change process has resulted in the creation of their own improvement system with a nationally recognized brand. The BICS improvement system has been applied to a wide range of patient pathways and supporting value streams with outstanding results. Their culture is now based on patient value supported with quality processes and motivated and skilled staff.

Leadership readily admits that they are just beginning their journey, but are well-equipped to make it a successful one.

The X Factor at Royal Bolton Hospital: An Even Balance between Tools and Culture

A key element in the effective implementation of Lean at Royal Bolton Hospital is balance: the even distribution of emphasis between Lean tools and culture. Fillingham recognized that success depended on true staff engagement—the culture portion of the equation—and also on the right application of BICS tools—the technical aspect. If the technical aspects of Lean implementation were emphasized at the expense of the cultural aspects, Fillingham believes it likely that BICS would be "owned" by just a few enthusiasts and any gains in efficiency would unlikely be sustained. There would consequently be no overall process transformation. At the other end of the spectrum, if the cultural aspects of Lean were the sole focus of implementation, it might result in better teamwork and higher levels of engagement with the change process, but the Trust would fail to reap the full potential of Lean transformation in terms of quality outcomes and financial improvements.

As a result, Fillingham emphasized a balanced approach to Lean implementation, drawing equally on the concepts, tools, and disciplines that comprise the technical aspects of Lean and on the cultural aspects of Lean, including the empowerment of Lean leadership within the organization and the full commitment of the board to Lean transformation. This balanced approach at the hospital has fueled the Trust's successful Lean transformation.

During the last year, the Trust has appointed a new chief executive, Lesley Doherty, who led much of the early development of BICS as chief operating officer of the organization. Following a consultation in spring 2010, it was announced that key services from NHS Bolton Primary Care Trust (PCT), and Royal Bolton NHS Foundation Trust (RBH), would be integrated from April 2011. The challenge in 2011 is to make this happen effectively. This is a unique opportunity to ensure leaders in both organizations gain sufficient understanding of the challenges going forward to lead such a transformation congruent with Lean principles. Lesley is now leading the integration of the Trust with the local community healthcare provider with the aim of creating the first Lean integrated care organization in the UK against the backdrop of delivering the challenges for the future, which include delivering the white paper "Liberating the NHS" while in an austere climate.

New York City Health and Hospitals Corporation: A Large Municipal System Transformation—A Work in Progress

4

A SNAPSHOT
of New York City Health and Hospitals Corporation

New York City Health and Hospitals Corporation (NYCHHC) is the largest municipal health system in the United States. With an operating budget of $6.3 billion, NYCHHC provides comprehensive healthcare services to 1.3 million New York City residents. Managing seventy-seven hundred beds, the corporation comprises eleven acute care hospitals, four skilled nursing facilities, six diagnostic and treatment centers, eighty community-based clinics, a certified home healthcare agency, and a managed care organization. Annually, NYCHHC provides two hundred and twenty-six thousand discharges and five million outpatient visits, including 1.1 million emergency room visits. More than one-third of the patients served at NYCHHC sites are uninsured.

The X-Factor at NYCHHC

The x-factor is the influence or quality that adds value and drives success.

Look for balance used to provide central office system oversight with local site autonomy

The Challenge

Any healthcare system CEO will tell you that changing the performance trajectory of a healthcare system is a daunting, uphill challenge—possible, but really, really hard work. Within a year of Lean adoption, NYCHHC CEO Alan D. Aviles was faced with an especially difficult situation: in a large municipal healthcare system whose mission is to provide care to New York City residents without regard to ability to pay; characterized by autonomous member hospitals; highly organized staff unions; a payer mix of 65 percent Medicaid; and a culturally and linguistically diverse patient population (one hundred and twenty different spoken languages), NYCHHC faced a budget gap of over $1.1 billion. Lean transformation, however, would be seen by Aviles and the other leaders of NYCHHC as an approach to not only surviving but thriving as a changed and stronger organization.

In the early 1990s, the NYCHHC was a disjointed system with a reputation for marginal quality of care and significant patient safety issues. In 1993, the Joint Commission denied accreditation for three member hospitals and gave conditional accreditation to a fourth. The organization was floundering fiscally as well. NYCHHC routinely ran at a deficit that totaled millions of dollars annually—overages passed on to the city each year. Difficulties and concerns mounted over the next several years. By the mid 1990s, Mayor Guiliani proposed closing the public hospitals and selling the facilities to private buyers. The sell-off was averted, but the crisis motivated NYCHHC executives to make significant changes.

Readying for Lean

Leaders jumped to work—reducing staff, shutting down nonessential clinical units, and closing unnecessary beds. They sponsored initiatives to improve efficiency and reduce average length of stay. Their efforts paid off. Costs were reined in and quality metrics improved. HHC issued its own bonds and received support from the city, initiating a capital improvement program in the mid-'90s to rebuild the physical and technological foundation of the organization. With this first injection of capital, which was followed by continued support from the subsequent mayor, Michael R. Bloomberg, leaders shored up the physical infrastructure with state-of-the-art ambulatory and acute care facilities and upgraded the enterprise-wide electronic health record. Using clinical collaboratives and teams of staff, NYCHHC boasted CMS core measure scores for their hospitals that surpassed many peer facilities in the region and across the country. The organization was recognized for innovation and quality of care, receiving the Codman, Pinnacle, and Davies awards, as well as achieving Magnet status recognition at Elmhurst Hospital Center. Mayor Michael Bloomberg remarked on the change, stating, "I am pleased to report that we are well on our way to making New York the healthiest city in the nation, and a big reason for our success has been our commitment to building the nation's most effective public hospital system."

Looking for Redesign—and Fast

NYCHHC central office leaders were no strangers to operational redesign. After successfully completing the Ambulatory Care Restructuring Initiative at all one hundred and thirty-seven primary care clinics in the system, visit cycle times were reduced by 50 percent, waits for appointments were reduced by 85 percent, and the no-show rate dropped by almost 60 percent. Importantly, leaders and staff saw that it was possible for improvement initiatives to be effective on an enterprise-wide scale. However, the initiative was "painfully slow" to show results, taking about six years, using an approach that lacked a sense of urgency and clear accountability for the sustained adoption of proven change strategies.

Although uniform changes were put in place across the system, the yield was uneven across the system. To move faster and deeper in its efforts to transform the system, and to ensure that gains could be sustained, a new, powerful improvement system was required.

The organization was successfully steering a new course when the national economic downturn struck in 2009. With the tightening of federal, state, and local budgets, and despite significant successful application of cost-reduction strategies, NYCHHC found itself with a 'perfect storm' of diminished support from its traditional sources of revenue while costs continued to rise. Suddenly, corporation leaders were looking at a projected one-billion-dollar deficit over the subsequent two years. They needed to find additional revenue and cost efficiencies, and become increasingly competitive quickly, at a level as yet unmatched by the system.

Leaders visited and communicated with other large health systems to learn about successful improvement initiatives. They were impressed by the work of Denver Health (see the chapter in this book), another municipal system with a commitment to serving all in need regardless of ability to pay. In November 2007, NYCHHC initiated implementation of Lean in the central office and across the entire hospital system.

Start-Up Challenges

NYCHHC leaders faced a number of serious challenges to "Breakthrough" (Lean) implementation before the very first event was even planned. First, despite the recent success of multiple clinical, operational, and financial improvement measures, there was lingering skepticism that a centrally managed, corporate-wide improvement initiative would work successfully in such a large, complex system. Second, the corporation was built on an organizational infrastructure subject to civil service rules and involving thirty-five unions and/or locals. Third, because of the fairly autonomous nature of the member hospitals, there was a sense of aversion to central control, especially with regard to mandated, standardized performance improvement initiatives. Finally, because NYCHHC is a municipal system with a publicly appointed CEO, leaders were uncertain that any improvement system would endure future political shifts in attention and focus.

Central office leaders addressed these challenges proactively. NYCHHC leaders met with union representatives at the inception of the "Breakthrough" initiative. The name "Breakthrough" was largely influenced by union representatives' concerns that 'patients aren't cars' (a reference to the

Toyota Production System). Union representatives were included in critical activities such as executive Breakthrough workshops and rapid improvement events. Leaders also invited union representatives to serve on various executive and value-stream steering committees.

"Breakthrough" champions were identified and emerged from the clinical and executive leadership within the system; their enthusiasm and early successes seeded interest and engagement among their peers. To address the political uncertainties of the system, NYCHHC leaders set their sights on embedding "Breakthrough" in the improvement and management infrastructure.

Site Adoption

One of the greatest challenges to "Breakthrough" implementation at NYCHHC was identifying the optimum process and sequence of "Breakthrough" adoption, site by site across such a vast system. Organizational leaders planned a uniform series of activities for each sequentially added site, with thirteen sites going live within the first two years. Site start-up was guided by the corporate "Breakthrough" office and preceded by educational opportunities, including planning and awareness sessions, suggested reading, and onsite observation of "Breakthrough" events at other sites.

Once these pre-implementation activities were completed and an initial core team of dedicated staff was on board, implementation could commence. The types of Lean activities, the sequence of activities, and the initial pace of implementation were consistent across the sites. After an introductory "Breakthrough" workshop with site leadership and union representatives, the site's senior team met in a two-day visioning workshop to clarify purpose and strategic goals for "Breakthrough" and to select two initial value streams. Within a month of this visioning workshop, the site would conduct a value-stream analysis (VSA) for each initial value stream. A primary product of the VSA was a plan for a series of RIEs, which were subsequently conducted at an initial pace of two per month (one in each value stream) beginning the third or fourth month post start-up. Over time and with the experience of several sites as a guide, new sites were guided to a pace that led gradually to an average of six events each month across between three and six value streams by the time the site reached twelve to eighteen months' maturity.

Early Experiences and Changes in Course

To ensure that "Breakthrough" resulted in value as defined by each site, and to foster rapid uptake of "Breakthrough," site leaders selected initial value streams. However, by the end of the first year, feeling the weight of the national recession and its impact on revenues and costs, NYCHHC leadership required that one of the initial value streams was either the emergency department or the operating room, because of the importance of these units for entry into the system and their significant impact on patient flow, revenue, and costs throughout the hospitals. At this time, November 2008, NYCHHC held an enterprise VSA to review progress to date and ensure that the focus of "Breakthrough" work continued to be relevant to the business of the organization. While results from the initial year were encouraging—for example, ten million dollars in cost savings and new revenue were achieved with seven sites engaged—leaders realized that "Breakthrough" efforts would need to continue at an accelerated pace if they were to maintain existing improvements and keep up with the increasingly tight economic situation. Financial experts estimated that by the end of 2009, the enterprise needed to achieve annual revenue and cost savings totaling one hundred million dollars.

Leaders reviewed the early experience with implementing Lean across the system. Initially, corporation leaders had planned to implement "Breakthrough" at twenty-two sites within three years, but found that effective launches cut out weeks or even months of slow and inefficient progress. Having added new sites more slowly than originally intended, the addition of sites in the second year allowed for the start-up of one to two sites in a quarter, and separated from the next launch by two to four months. This spacing provided necessary time for new starts to appreciate and recruit the optimum staffing structure and characteristics. Sites were encouraged to hire dedicated "Breakthrough" staff from within in order to provide promotional opportunities and gain the site expertise of existing staff. In addition, this timeframe allowed the senior leadership team of each site to observe and participate in pre-implementation learning and mobilization activities.

According to Chief Innovation Officer Omi, effective spread strategies continue to be one of the corporation's highest priorities. "We're experimenting right now with how to replicate success from one facility, while maintaining the individuality of each site. We know that you can't just say, 'Here, they did this at Metropolitan, so you've got to do the same at Woodhull.' So we're experimenting with what the communication and support needs to be in order to transfer the learning from one site to another." To support the spread of validated improvements, in the third year, the enterprise steering committee, comprised of the president and senior site and corporate office executives, developed a yokoten plan that supports the adoption of learning and improvement from site to site and from enterprise-level work throughout the system.

In the first year, the enterprise vision for "Breakthrough" was far-reaching, encompassing stretch goals for quality, safety, patient and staff satisfaction, and efficiency goals. A year later, the leadership revised these goals, making them more targeted toward their emerging financial priorities. Still, identifying metrics that related directly to the aggregate achievements of site and enterprise improvement work proved difficult, and, in part, this was a function of the early decision to support site autonomy in value-stream selection. By the end of the second year, more than thirty value streams were producing results that, with the exception of financial outputs, could not be clearly linked to enterprise metrics. More work was needed to ensure that value-stream and RIE activity was guided by enterprise and site priorities. Similarly, following driver metrics from the level of RIE activity through value-stream metrics and ultimately to an associated enterprise metric could not be done across all dimensions of "Breakthrough" work as the enterprise metrics were in constant flux.

The enterprise steering committee worked to better align Breakthrough work at the site level with system-level work. They also set specific revenue goals for the system and re-doubled their efforts to realistically assess the financial impact of each RIE. For example, Marlene Zurack, the corporate chief financial officer, worked with each site CFO to develop standards for monetizing events. NYCHHC leaders also adopted more focused goals for system-wide improvement, including initiatives for enterprise-wide charge capture, materials management, and the implementation of new work flows for the financial information system being developed. They engaged a Simpler project manager in the central office to help plan enterprise-wide strategic initiatives and review site-level progress toward transformational goals.

Full engagement of site leadership was critically important and had a huge impact on the success of Breakthrough efforts. Events, including an annual conference and regular reports by sites to the corporate board of directors, provided forums for sharing successes and learning from leading edge sites. The work of process owners—those individuals responsible for the implementation and sustaining of RIE team improvements—was supported by the introduction of one-day training sessions aimed at role clarification and the provision of tools, including standard work.

Results

As of June 2010, more than four hundred RIEs have been conducted, with almost five thousand individuals participating in some form of Breakthrough activity and more than twenty-five hundred engaged in RIEs and VSAs. Sixty-seven million dollars in cost savings and new revenue has resulted from these efforts. Although this is not the one hundred million hoped for by the end of the second year, NYCHHC is well on its way to achieving this amount on an annualized basis. According to NYCHHC President and CEO Alan D. Aviles, Lean has been instrumental in changing the financial picture for the municipal system. "At this time of unprecedented pressures on NYCHHC, the Breakthrough initiative continues to provide us with a strong and successful process to reduce waste and achieve clinical and operational efficiencies that are measurable and sustainable."

Leaders realized that to achieve lasting improvements and embed a permanent structure for improvement into the hospital system, they needed to "go deep rather than wide." They need to ensure that process owners have sufficient time and resources to conduct follow-up activities after each RIE. They need to guard against burnout of the enthusiastic. For long-term, sustainable success, system leaders are now budgeting more time to achieve complete roll-out and meet enterprise goals than they initially estimated. NYCHHC leaders are willing to make these shifts because they see Breakthrough as a way to grow a cadre of problem-solvers who can create truly effective solutions from the frontlines of care.

Conclusion

NYCHHC is a large and complex municipal hospital system that was ready for a new, powerful improvement system that would accelerate transformation Two years ago, system leaders adopted Lean as a means for ensuring institutional capacity to perform to its mission in an increasingly competitive and volatile environment. In just two years, NYCHHC leaders have built a foundation for cultural change, begun enterprise-wide transformation, increased revenues and reduced costs, and developed an effective process for achieving even greater cost efficiency and revenue generation in the future.

The X-Factor at NYCHHC: A Balance between Local Site Autonomy and Central Direction

Executives planned for consistent initiation and delivery across sites and created early support materials centrally to ensure uniform training and uptake. Yet, central office leaders believed that site autonomy for certain decisions—the specific value streams chosen initially, for example—fostered ownership of transformation within their individual sites and avoided the cultural resistance that might have developed if all aspects of Lean implementation had been mandated by corporation leaders.

An effective balance between site autonomy and central office oversight was believed to be essential to success by Alan D. Aviles, president and CEO. Aviles expected Breakthrough would thrive under the creative and experienced management of local leaders. Aviles' personal engagement in Lean transformation set an expectation of full engagement by executive leaders at each NYCHHC site at which Lean has been implemented. In addition, the corporation's chief innovation officer, Joanna Omi, supported the development of effective local infrastructure and provided training on the enterprise improvement model. Through frequent on-site visits and communication, Omi ensured that leaders of sites across the organization were following and implementing the Lean approach and tools consistently.

St. Joseph Health System: Actualizing a Faith-Based Mission

The X-Factor at St. Joseph

The x-factor is the influence or quality that adds value and drives success.

Look for a Lean system aligned to the Sisters of St. Joseph mission and called "The St. Joseph Way"

A History of Service

St. Joseph Health System (SJHS) traces its roots to a Jesuit priest in seventeenth-century France. Jean-Pierre Medaille organized the Sisters of St. Joseph to minister to the needs of the local community. In 1912, a contingent of the order established a school in Eureka, California, and in 1920, answering a need to respond to the influenza epidemic of 1918, founded St. Joseph Hospital, the first healthcare facility of the health system.

Mission remains the central driving force for SJHS. Leaders are guided in their quest to deliver compassionate care and improve health and quality of life in the communities they serve by the organization's three mission outcomes: Sacred Encounters, Perfect Care, and Healthiest Communities.

Sacred Encounters refers to the organization's commitment to honoring the dignity of each person and creating an environment infused with compassion and care for others. Staff and leaders are called to act on this goal by embodying compassion in every encounter they have with patients, family members, and other employees.

Perfect Care refers to the organization's quest to provide the highest possible quality of care that is both patient-centered and evidence-based. It reflects the organization's commitment to performance improvement and to the pursuit of excellence in clinical quality, patient safety, and patient satisfaction.

Healthiest Communities is the SJHS commitment to improving the health of the residents within the communities served by each of its ministries. The goal is actualized in several public health initiatives and collaborations in the community. One example is a campaign to address childhood obesity, which includes a physical education program within local schools and nutrition education for families.

The Need to Drive Change

In the pursuit of these goals, SJHS leaders were becoming increasingly concerned about the results of performance metrics. All fourteen of the organization's ministries were engaged in some form of performance improvement. Yet no two ministries applied the same approach. Some used Focus Plan-Do-Check-Act (PDCA) cycles. Others favored Plan-Do-Study-Act (PDSA) cycles. And still others integrated a three-question model from the Institute for Healthcare Improvement. Furthermore, among the ministries that used the same model, their approach to applying it varied considerably. The result was a dramatic difference in the way performance improvement initiatives were initiated, run, monitored, and sustained at the ministries. Not surprisingly, this variability was evident in the ministries' publicly reported metrics, such as CMS core measures, which differed across the health system. When health system leaders investigated the variability, they found that the involvement of ministry leadership and the methods used to drive improvement—and the degree of success—were inconsistent. Underlying this issue was that ministry departments unknowingly supported work-arounds rather than root-cause problem-solving.

In addition, leaders believed that the industry was demanding more efficiency and patient-focused care and that SJHS could better deliver on its core mission of improving the health and quality of life of residents served in their local communities. Convinced of the need for change, executives knew they were challenged by the geography of SJHS—an organization with more than a dozen healthcare entities located over wide and differing regions. Yet they wanted to foster a more standardized approach to performance improvement in all ministries despite their differences. And they wanted to bring together all these entities to deliver effectively on the SJHS mission.

System leaders were skeptical of consulting firms that typically provide diagnostic support and short-term solutions but fail to trigger the deep organizational shifts necessary for lasting change. They wanted something different, an approach that would both unify the system and become embedded within it, promoting change that would outlive any single improvement initiative. They wanted an approach that would show rapid results *and* be long-lasting. They decided to try Lean.

In May 2007, system leaders engaged Simpler Healthcare to help address their organization's performance variability. St. Mary Medical Center (SMMC) was the pilot site. Located in the town of Apple Valley in Southern California, the medical center includes a one-hundred-and-eighty-six-bed acute care hospital, an outpatient surgery pavilion, and several community health centers. Once the engagement appeared to be working at SMMC, system leaders decided to expand and include the entire health system.

Deployment and Acceleration

Over the course of eighteen months, health system leadership introduced the Lean approach at all care entities within the system. The initiative was named the "St. Joseph Way" to emphasize the importance of the culture transformation central to the new process for change—a new "way" of doing things. Rather than attempting to employ Lean at all sites simultaneously, health system leaders decided to stagger the implementation. Leaders worked with Simpler *sensei* to determine the ideal pace for rollout: sufficiently measured to allow health system executives and program leaders to provide support, but fast enough to achieve momentum.

Although a basic tenet of Lean is *rapid* improvement, effective rapid improvement events (RIEs) required several months of prep work: time for planning, building the system for improvement, developing a Transformation Plan of Care[SM] (TPOC), training the core team, and conducting a value-stream analysis (VSA). Some ministry leaders were very interested in Lean and wanted to jump in immediately, but ultimately a controlled pace of rollout was adopted to ensure steady learning and effective implementation of the St. Joseph Way at each ministry. To capitalize on valuable clinician and employee enthusiasm, health system leaders worked with local ministry leadership and executive sponsors to develop an overall initial plan for the rollout at each ministry. Later, these individuals served as knowledgeable resources for others in the ministry.

Because of the difficulty in rolling out a standardized process for change at geographically distant—and demographically diverse—locations, Simpler *sensei* were assigned to each ministry. The *sensei* spent one week each month at their assigned ministry, working with executive management to introduce the St. Joseph Way, including developing local ministry priorities, launching the initial value streams, coaching executive leaders, and teaching and mentoring facilitators. Assigning a *sensei* to each ministry provided consistency in the planned rollout and ensured that competency development and coaching would continue throughout the rollout period. It also helped establish a cadence for Lean-related events. If a *sensei* was assigned to a ministry for a particular week of the month, it was expected that planned events would occur that week as scheduled, regardless of external circumstances. It also was expected that once a rhythm for improvement events was set, the pace of change would continue.

Getting Started

After the local executive team created the ministry level TPOC, a guiding document integrating elements of the strategic plan as well as prioritized functional areas called value streams, then executive sponsors were assigned to the value streams. Executive sponsors initiated collaboration with involved department managers, clinicians, and other employees to identify problematic areas in the current process. Development of a plan called a value-stream analysis identified RIEs, projects, and tasks to address the problems and gaps while moving the ministry toward a target state. The value stream was conducted over the subsequent twelve to eighteen months. At each ministry, a core team of about five individuals was selected to work on the initial value streams. The team was held accountable for overseeing the work on the value stream from start to finish, ensuring progress at a reasonable pace while improvements were sustained and any barriers were resolved as quickly as possible with the help of the executive sponsor.

System leaders worked with Simpler *sensei* to initiate the St. Joseph Way at additional ministries between 2007 and 2009. The number of ministries involved and the pace of activity accelerated over time (see table).

Year	FY 2007	FY 2008	FY 2009	FY 2010 (6 mos)
Number of ministries using St. Joseph Way	7	10	12	12
Number of value streams run	13	17	26	30
Number of Rapid Improvement Events	6	140	152	156
Number of individuals who participated in an event	160	940	1200	735

A key element in the successful implementation at SJHS was proactive identification of the technical and cultural barriers to meaningful improvement. Among the barriers typically identified were leadership's level of engagement, the need for more widespread training in Lean, and the acceptance of standard work across the system.

Engaging Leaders

At the initiation of the St. Joseph Way in 2007, the amount of engagement among ministry leaders varied widely. Some leaders were well aware of performance issues in their hospitals and eager to accept Lean. Others were reluctant to begin what they perceived as "yet another performance improvement initiative." A few leaders, whose ministries were achieving superior performance metrics, were reticent to make changes when their results were already first-rate.

To better inform and influence leadership engagement, the health system created metrics to monitor progress in various value streams across the system, using quarterly reports to quantify the degree of improvement achieved for each value stream. The dashboard also included metrics that reflected return on mission and return on investment. According to health system leaders, the tool has helped ministry leaders appreciate the power of Lean in transforming culture and impacting performance.

Another essential element in engaging leaders, especially those with high performance metrics, was the move toward transparency. The *sensei* introduced tools to make "invisible" problems more obvious. Tools such as standard work documents, production control boards, and information centers clearly showed where practices deviated from the ideal. With a transparent work environment, leaders were more inclined to become actively involved and help support frontline staff in identifying and addressing problems. Another factor that influenced leadership was the level of engagement and excitement demonstrated by frontline staff when given the tools and empowerment to effect change.

Addressing Training Needs

Implementing Lean necessitated the adoption of a new way of considering work, required new skills, and demanded the use of new tools and unfamiliar terminology. This need for widespread training in basic and advanced Lean concepts and tools posed some challenges. To address the knowledge and competency gaps, health system leaders designed several educational interventions. A series of four-hour education workshops was created for key executive ministry team members, including chief executive, operating, nursing, and financial officers, as well the leaders of information systems and human resources. During the first four or five months, the health system also sponsored a series of workshops on the St. Joseph Way for the vice presidents of mission integration. Later, leaders worked with Simpler to develop a Green Belt program. The week-long training included experiential simulations and hands-on exercises, as well as theory and application of Lean tools. To become Green Belt certified, an individual must attend the course and pass the "open book" test, participate in one RIE, then subsequently lead an RIE and sustain the results. Once members of the executive ministry team became Green Belt certified, upper- and middle-management began to take the course. During 2009, the health system created a more advanced training course called Black Belt. To be accepted into the week-long course, individuals must have led, facilitated, or participated in at least six RIEs. Once completing the week-long Black Belt course and the "open book" test, individuals were required to facilitate a Black Belt project, which is an initiative that advances the St. Joseph Way within their ministry and is approved by the *sensei* and the executive sponsor in their ministry.

The health system also sponsored a facilitator development program that included monthly conference calls for facilitators throughout the health system and a twice yearly three- to five-day facilitator development course. These courses were a blend of experiential activities, training in Lean tools, and the sharing of best practices. Each facilitator developed a personal A3 with a skills matrix to foster and track competency. After four years at the facilitator level, individuals are expected to display sufficient competency to step into an advanced facilitator role. Health system and ministry leaders were also given opportunities to learn directly from leaders of other organizations that have successfully implemented Lean. In 2009, executive leaders convened a team to tour both medical centers and non-healthcare companies to observe their use of Lean.

From the beginning stages through today, system leaders worked on a comprehensive communication plan to educate and inform ministry leaders and staff about Lean and current activities and opportunities. At the beginning stages of roll-out, a system-wide communication plan was launched that included introduction of the branded name "The St. Joseph Way," along with key messages, presentations, and articles about the purpose of Lean and how it would be initiated across the system. A system-wide newsletter, called *Milestones*, was created for leadership and staff that highlights progress made by each local ministry on the St. Joseph Way journey, provides education about Lean tools and practices, profiles facilitators supporting local ministry efforts, and shares best practices and quotes from the frontline clinician and employee experiences in RIEs.

Introducing Standard Work

Organizational leaders found it was essential to standardize the roles of frontline managers and hold staff accountable for standard work. The *sensei* encouraged the use of Lean tools to reinforce and support the performance of standard work. Teams at local ministries developed visual management boards and information centers with displayed metrics comparing expected and observed work patterns to support standard work of frontline staff. In addition, facilitators created standard work plans for the frontline managers and executives (such as a standardized list of items for executives to assess on walk rounds) to help these leaders oversee and support the St. Joseph Way in a consistent fashion. Although health system leaders recognized the importance of standard work, they also appreciated the need for local customization allowing each ministry to tailor certain aspects of Lean application to their particular needs and resources.

To foster the long-term use of standard work, health system leaders recently launched a pilot at one of the ministries that is focused on sustainment—understanding deeply what it means to sustain improvements. Helpful tools, coaching, and mentoring support were all developed to ensure that favorable outcomes were upheld. The lessons gleaned from this pilot will be spread to other ministries across the health system.

Convergence: St. Joseph Way and the Three Strategic Goals

Initially, health system leaders considered the idea of referring to the Lean initiative as the "Lean Improvement System." Upon further reflection, they chose the moniker "The St. Joseph Way." The name proved to be fitting: over time, the leaders realized that the Lean approach was not only a means for transforming the organization's culture and improving performance, but also of better aligning daily work with the health system's three mission outcomes. According to Mary Kingston, vice president of performance improvement for the health system, "All the events initiated across SJHS are driven by our desire to achieve Sacred Encounters, Perfect Care, and Healthiest Communities. It's a way to more mindfully connect each event and the work that we do every day with the mission and values of the St. Joseph Health System."

Health system leaders now encourage the ministry executives to use the St. Joseph Way to address gaps in meeting system goals. RIE participants are asked to consider any barriers, redundancy, waste, or other problem that might prevent the consistent delivery of Sacred Encounters, Perfect Care, and Healthiest Communities. Just as a filter placed on a camera lens shifts the photograph's image, the careful, detailed consideration of strategic goals shifts the way teams approach, run, and experience RIEs. To reinforce use of the "lens," system leaders comment and reflect on the strategic goals during the weekly RIE debriefings that are presented. Querying participants about the potential effects of a process change on Sacred Encounters, for example, reinforces the overriding importance of attaining strategic goals. After these sessions, ministry leaders, clinicians, and employees return to their work with a renewed passion for change and a stronger connection to the mission.

Health system leaders also have emphasized the importance of standard work across the organization. SJHS leaders and Simpler *sensei* likened the shift to standard work to using a recipe when baking: if a good cake recipe is followed every time, the likely result is consistently a good cake; if you deviate from the recipe, the result may be less than desirable. Similarly, by ensuring that clinical, administrative, and other work processes are performed in standardized ways, consistent outcomes are more likely—even in areas where metric results are already favorable.

Fostering a New Kind of Leadership

Over time, the St. Joseph Way has "matured," and leaders have shifted from focusing almost exclusively on RIEs to focusing equal attention on sustaining the changes made during RIE weeks. System leaders learned through experience that active leadership involvement was an absolute necessity for sustaining gains. In becoming actively involved, leaders were required to learn to lead in new ways, rejecting "old style" leadership that kept them in their offices and instead sought the direct input for frontline clinicians and employees. To truly understand these implications, leaders need a clear, accurate picture of the frontline work flow.

Health system leaders began developing a whole new set of skills: listening to managers and employees, and supporting them in solving problems demonstrating the new way of leading with *gemba* walks. "Gemba" is a Japanese term that translates as "the actual place." During their *gemba* walks, leaders toured the frontline workplace, querying the clinicians and employees about current practices and improvement initiatives and looking for even more opportunities for improvement. Eventually, the *gemba* walk became a powerful tool for increasing engagement at all levels of the organization. By example, ministry executives demonstrated to ministry directors and managers how to use *gemba* walks to better understand the improvement needs of their departments while emphasizing to frontline clinicians appreciation of their work. Today, the walks are now conducted by both system and ministry leaders on a regular basis.

Another change occurred in the way metrics were selected and used. Early in the Lean journey, many metrics were selected. However, with too many metrics, it was found that most didn't provide meaningful or relevant insights. Over time, only a select few metrics were chosen, matching them carefully with the RIE to ensure that the event had the potential to drive improvements being measured. For example, an RIE to improve the scheduling process in the cardiac catheterization lab would be unlikely to drive improvement in adherence to evidence-based care, such as administration of aspirin on arrival for patients with acute myocardial infarction. Instead, the event would be more likely to drive change in the time available for scheduling, room turnover, and patient throughput. Having just a few key metrics was essential to sustaining gains in improvement.

Cultural Transformation and Performance Breakthroughs

Senior leadership is committed to the St. Joseph Way and recognized that in order to respond to industry and patient demands for a patient-focused experience with better outcomes at lower costs, and in order to deliver on the mission outcomes, St. Joseph Health System needed a cultural transformation. They realized that creating a culture of performance improvement required a new approach, and one that truly engaged leadership and employees, providing them with the tools and skills to make change happen. "We have seen the signs of the times and responded to them, consistent with the history of the Sisters of St. Joseph of Orange," says Deborah Proctor, president and CEO. "The St. Joseph Way has provided an opportunity to proactively shape our future in a way that is values based and focused on supporting our three goals of Perfect Care, Sacred Encounters, and Healthiest Communities."

Leaders have seen the impact of the St. Joseph Way as well, noting the "pull" of employees to participate in RIEs and be involved in Green Belt Trainings, as well as the enthusiasm that has been generated among staff. Being empowered to change their work processes, feeling supported by managers with new skills, and seeing the impact of the changes made on patient care and the work environment has energized short- and long-term employees. This is demonstrated by a sampling of quotes from employees that have been highlighted in the "Heard in the Halls" section of the St. Joseph Way newsletter, *Milestones*:

> "I think every employee should be in an RIE. It was a great experience and helps employees welcome change." - Local ministry staff RN

> "It's all about developing new skills and habits...and I am a believer in this process—it works!" - Local ministry COO

> "This performance improvement approach seems to be working the best of what I have seen in my career and I am thrilled with the excitement and engagement of staff." - Local ministry CEO

> "You just have to experience one [RIE] to understand it...hard to describe, but amazing." - Local ministry facilitator

"Before I was on the team, I thought the RIE was just a way to get us to do more and work harder. Now I realize the goal is to make things better!" - Local ministry environmental services worker

"The one thing I hear from staff who have participated in the RIE is that it was both the hardest week they ever had and the most rewarding week they ever had while working here." - Local ministry chief medical officer

"We accomplished some things that have been big elephants in the room for years and years." - Local ministry RN

"This has experience has been like the quote from Confucious – *"If you tell me, I will forget. If you show me, I will remember. If you involve me, I WILL DO!"* - System leader

As more staff became involved in the St. Joseph Way, the level of cultural transformation has grown. The journey is not a short one, nor is it complete. However, the transformation desired has gained momentum as more departments have participated and more RIEs have been completed.

Although it is difficult to determine if these efforts have driven increases in overall patient and employee satisfaction, there are many examples of improvements in specific department satisfaction at ministries where St. Joseph Way efforts have been concentrated. At one ministry, St. Joseph Hospital Eureka, efforts on a PCU monitored care unit have not only transformed patient flow and work processes, but have resulted in patient satisfaction reaching close to the ninety-fifth percentile and staff morale improving significantly. "This was a unit where we had difficulty retaining clinical leadership, and now clinical leaders are asking to be assigned to that unit," comments the hospital's COO, Bob Brannigan.

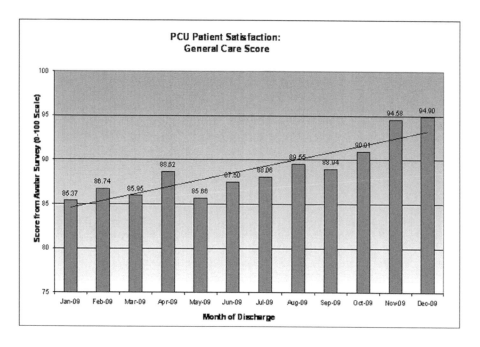

Similarly, Covenant Health System, a SJHS ministry based in Texas, has seen dramatic results since starting the St. Joseph Way over two years ago. In their second year, Covenant conducted fifty-two RIEs and has increased sustainment of tracked metrics from 27 to 85 percent, achieving savings of more than six million dollars.

System-wide, in FY 2009 more than one hundred and fifty RIEs were conducted with more than twelve hundred staff members participating. Process changes and productivity improvements resulted in more than twelve million dollars in cost savings, with more than one hundred thousand hours in patient time saved and more than one hundred and seventy thousand hours of FTE time saved through the reduction of non-valued added activities. Probably more importantly, changes are occurring in skills, practices, and attitudes—in essence a culture shift towards addressing problems and working together to achieve performance improvement and organizational goals. This journey at St. Joseph Health System has shown that it is possible to achieve cultural shift and performance improvement; in fact, the latter relies on the former.

Looking to the Future

By fully engaging ministry leaders, providing widespread Lean training, and fostering the development of standardized processes, St. Joseph Health System leaders have effectively implemented Lean across a geographically and demographically diverse organization. Along the way, the leaders realized that the St. Joseph Way not only transformed the organization's culture and improved performance, but also helped the organization better deliver on its mission by aligning daily work with the health system's three mission outcomes: Sacred Encounters, Perfect Care, and Healthiest Communities. Relying on a framework for positive cultural change, in the form of the St. Joseph Way, health system leaders leveraged the strong mission that binds its component ministries and paved the way for reaching its goals today and far into the future.

The X-Factor at St. Joseph Health System: Mission and Values

Mission and values are central to the culture and organization of St. Joseph Health System. Although its operations span more than fourteen distinct subsidiaries and three different states, a common set of values—dignity, service, excellence, and justice—permeates the culture and are embraced by employees across the system. Consistently employees credit a shared commitment to these values and the mission of "improving health and quality of life of the people in the communities served" as a driver in their loyalty to the organization. The mission gives meaning and purpose to the delivery of healthcare, which as an industry has become more like big business than a calling. Driven by its faith-based mission, St. Joseph Health System strives to "keep the faith" in how it operates and delivers its services.

Tan Tock Seng Hospital: Leveraging Improvement Experience and Know-How

A SNAPSHOT
of Tan Tock Seng Hospital

Established in 1844, Tan Tock Seng Hospital (TTSH) is the second largest hospital in Singapore. Recognized as an industry leader in providing world-class care, the twelve-hundred--bed, not-for-profit hospital is part of the National Healthcare Group (NHG), an integrated network of public healthcare facilities. In addition to comprehensive healthcare services, the acute care general hospital offers specialty centers in rehabilitation medicine and communicable diseases. TTSH was the first hospital in Singapore to open a civilian hyperbaric chamber, the first in Southeast Asia to provide macular translocation surgery, and the first in Asia to offer vision restoration therapy for partial blindness from stroke and traumatic brain injury. The hospital is accredited by Joint Commission International and achieved Singapore Quality Class, a designation that recognizes high performance in "the journey to business excellence."

The X-Factor at Tan Tock Seng Hospital

The x-factor is the influence or quality that adds value and drives success.

Look for an integration of Lean thinking to existing pervasive culture of improvement

The Case for Change

Unlike many healthcare organizations in the world today, the primary motivation for Lean implementation at Tan Tock Seng Hospital (TTSH) was not financial necessity. Instead, the burning platform for TTSH leaders was capacity—the hospital's physical capacity was not keeping pace with demand for services as the country's population aged rapidly. TTSH leaders were concerned that the high patient-to-staff ratios would climb and compromise quality as well as overwhelm employees, prompting staff to seek employment elsewhere. Complicating the issue, length of stay and treatment times were unacceptably high. Hospital leadership accepted the challenge of providing care to more patients without expanding the physical capacity. At the same time, Tan Tock Seng leaders wanted to ensure that, while increasing capacity and productivity, the organization maintained its high-quality standards and its reputation as a worldwide healthcare leader.

Continuous Improvement Was Not New to TTSH

A decade ago, TTSH leaders launched their continuous process improvement plan (CPIP), a project-based improvement program. The CPIP initiative allowed staff to make significant improvements in discrete sections of various processes, but had limited effect on the overall design of important patient care processes. Professor Philip Choo, chairman of the TTS Medical Board and a world-renowned expert in performance benchmarking and Lean healthcare practices, sums it up best when he says, "There are many steps in a healthcare process; if you only make significant progress in one step, that results in only a little effect to the patient."

Leaders recognized that a broad-based improvement strategy was needed to allow them to make comprehensive, yet rapid, changes to processes throughout the hospital. External training and peer networking convinced TTSH leaders to seriously consider the application of Lean principles and techniques. They began applying Lean tools at TTSH in 2006. After several months, executive leaders, including then-NHG Chief Executive Officer Dr. Lim Suet Wun, realized that despite the hard work, results at TTSH were not as robust as those of peer organizations that were applying Lean. Admittedly consultant-averse, the leaders at TTSH recognized they needed help and in January 2007 decided to use external Lean experts.

Developing Self-Sufficiency

Initially, external Lean support was on site at TTSH for one week each month for a twelve-month engagement. External support included teaching and coaching of Lean activities, including value-stream analysis (VSA), rapid improvement events (RIEs), and transformation plan of care (TPOC) reviews. Leaders and staff members were trained. Lean experts also provided hands-on coaching and teaching for leaders and staff during Lean implementation. Leaders and staff worked closely in earnest on Lean implementation.

TTSH leaders also created a vision and future plan for the hospital. They identified and set targets for the hospital's True North metrics: quality, timeliness, costs, and human

development. TTHS named their Lean improvement system MyCare. MyCare is built on a long-standing patient-centric culture that emphasizes the individual responsibility of each employee to consider the value of any action, service, or product provided to the patient. It places importance and focus on "faster, better, cheaper, and safer" care by developing leaders, enhancing staff skills and capabilities, and building effective systems and teams. MyCare also highlights the critical importance of staff satisfaction and retention. The system provides support through improved processes in human resources, information technology, and facilities management. To avoid potential problems with misalignment, leaders were careful to integrate MyCare with the existing project-based improvement program at the hospital, CPIP.

Developing a Hospital-Wide Inclusive Culture

In February 2008, hospital leaders created a MyCare "benefits tracker," a comparative dashboard that identifies and monitors the True North metrics in terms of providing **"faster, better,**

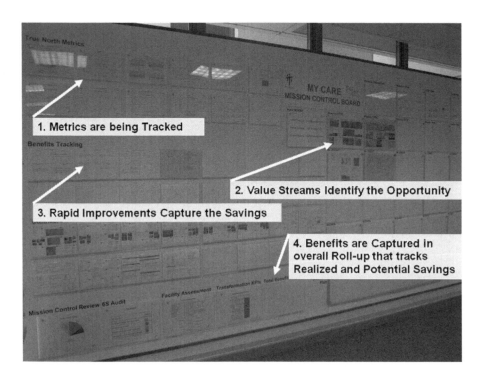

cheaper, and safer" care (see figure). According to Professor Choo, MyCare is the framework within which staff can effectively apply Lean and other improvement tools.

Prior to rolling out Lean, TTSH leaders recognized the need to implement the MyCare approach simultaneously on three different levels. Implementation needed to include "top-down" initiatives to engage leadership. It needed to include "bottom-up" activities, such as 6S and problem-solving events, to change culture at the frontlines. Finally, to sustain gains in improvement, implementation needed to include the "middle management," with active participation of department supervisors.

To create the Future State vision for the whole hospital and identify priority areas for improvement, TTSH conducted an enterprise-wide value-stream analysis. In this analysis, leaders and staff focused on the frontlines of care to clearly understand current processes and to identify the needs of customers in each service line. Using the PDCA cycle and Lean tools, they introduced revised processes, checked their progress toward providing value to customers, and then revised the processes again to incorporate what they had learned. Using this iterative method, leaders and staff evaluated and improved both clinical and nonclinical processes throughout the organization, working on twenty different value streams over the course of two years. Because of the organizational need for increased throughput and capacity, many of the value streams related to the efficient use of facilities. Staff and leaders ran RIEs for each value stream to identify specific changes to improve efficiency and release capacity. Using the Benefits Tracker, leaders were able to quantify potential improvement and track realized benefits.

Reaping Rewards in Discharge

Because the hospital needed to operate at greater efficiency, optimizing discharge was a critical priority. Therefore, one of the first value streams TTSH staff and leaders tackled was the discharge process. Leaders sought to maximize the discharge process so that flow out of the hospital corresponded to the need for patient beds. This goal entailed ensuring that discharges occur just as efficiently on weekends as weekdays and that discharges take place earlier in the day, countering the end-of-day back-up in the emergency department. According to Professor Choo, a key step was understanding that the tasks associated with discharge are predictable and can be standardized. He notes, "About eighty percent of the time we can identify a patient's length of stay within twenty-four hours of admission. So, we can spread out the discharge tasks over time. Plus we can let the patient and families know about the planned discharge, so that discharges can occur throughout the day and can be mapped to the need for beds." Through an iterative process of sequential rapid improvement events (REIs), the team identified and addressed bottlenecks and other problems in the discharge process.

Prior to implementing Lean, staff generally avoided making discharge decisions on weekends for patients they were cross-covering. Other weekend problems included delays in clinical assessment, unclear discharge instructions, transportation issues, and lack of advanced notice to family members. To address these problems, the value-stream team developed a more standardized procedure for discharge planning and focused on improving the availability of the estimated discharge date (EDD) for each patient. In addition to improving team communication though more nursing involvement in the discharge process, they also created visual boards to track patients' EDD and date of discharge activities.

By making small changes over time, the Lean team and staff achieved substantial improvements. The proportion of patients discharged before 1:00 p.m. doubled from 15 to 32 percent hospital-wide and the number of discharges on Sundays improved by 10 to 15 percent. As a result of the change in discharge pattern, emergency department dwell time declined. According to Dr. Endean Tan, a member of the discharge value stream team, "Initially the main problem we faced was one of poor compliance; inertia is comforting, and a new system is not always the easiest thing to implement. However, the results have been eminently encouraging, and our medical staff is starting to see huge benefits."

This significant improvement in discharge performance resulted in a dramatic reduction in the adjusted length of stay from twelve to eight days.

Level 11 Wards: Overall Discharge Pattern

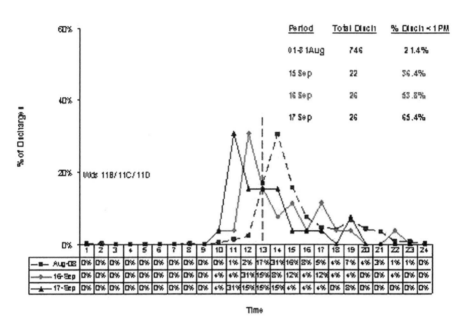

Figure: showing key shift in discharge pattern

Overhauling the Short Stay Process

During the initial visioning workshops for the MyCare program, data analysis also showed that by making even a half-day improvement in short stay conditions, this would release considerable capacity. Therefore creating a short stay unit and improving short stay processes became another important value stream for TTSH. Rather than running a value stream on short stay processes for each clinical diagnosis/ condition, hospital leaders decided to run a single value-stream event to improve processes across all relevant diagnoses/conditions within the department (notably the general surgery department). To sustain improvements, they also set up a dedicated short stay unit. The advantage of the strategy was that the changes needed were identified and implemented quickly. As Professor Choo notes, "It took six months to do this project, rather than the years it would have taken if we had done each as a separate value stream."

Current state analysis on the short stay process revealed a number of key issues:

- Sixty-seven percent of general surgery (GS) patients had a length of stay of three days or less, yet total flow time for a GS patient from admission to discharge could range from twenty-four to two hundred and forty hours, with length of stay for the department averaging above four days.
- Wait time for a bed could go beyond ten hours.
- Patients made over twenty stops during the course of travel from admission to treatment (i.e., surgery).
- Staff completed more than forty different forms during the entire process for each patient.

Having studied the Toyota Production System, Professor Choo borrowed insights from their effective assembly line procedures. MyCare focused on increasing throughput in a new dedicated short stay unit by making four overall process changes:

- Reducing procedure time and time for investigation by healthcare providers
- Providing a short-track discharge option (an automated system by which nurses can discharge patients)
- Shortening the time it takes for a senior physician to make a patient-care management decision, and
- Consolidating the processes by using standard care pathways, where applicable.

By implementing specific changes identified in a series of RIEs, the team achieved significant improvements:

- Length of stay was reduced by 12 to 43 percent across different conditions.
- Readmission rates were maintained.

- Turnaround time for key tests like ultrasound/CT scans improved by 37 percent.
- Staff satisfaction generally improved due to enhanced empowerment and workflows.

Spreading MyCare across the Hospital

TTSH staff and leaders addressed many other value streams as a result of the enterprise-wide value stream analysis, including processes for hip fracture treatment, repositioning of clinics to maximize available space, and improving patient flow through specific clinical care units. Because of the hospital's space constraints, many of the value-stream activities related to the repositioning and redesign of patient clinics. Using the Mycare redesign process, leaders and staff were able to improve patient flow, increase efficiency, and reduce wait times in both inpatient and ambulatory clinics throughout the hospital.

Although CEO Lim cautioned, "It is too early in our Lean journey to have quantitative feedback from staff and patients," he reports that the qualitative response to Lean-associated changes from both constituents has been positive.

Overcoming Barriers

According to Lim, TTSH leaders faced several barriers as they implemented the Mycare approach. They needed to obtain adequate buy-in to MyCare from senior management. They needed to prevent potential "turf issues" that would hamper the change process. TTSH leaders also needed to address the trepidation and unease staff felt when faced with an unfamiliar process and new tools, in spite of their performance improvement culture.

TTSH leaders used several strategies to overcome these hurdles. They ensured that senior management was visibly involved in the various activities associated with MyCare. They focused significant attention on staff education about MyCare. They launched a monthly newsletter written by executive staff about recent Lean-related activities. The newsletter includes many quotes from staff members about their personal experience with Lean activities. They also worked to ensure synergy between the existing performance improvement program (CPIP) and MyCare, thus avoiding confusion about priorities and conflicting alignment. Leaders also utilized a train-the-trainer model for educating staff in the use of 6S. By spreading knowledge about the process widely, hospital leaders were able to implement fifteen different 6S projects over a relatively short span of time.

Looking to the Future

The future goals of TTSH leaders include ensuring sustainment of gains achieved to date and expanding the direct involvement of executives in value-stream analysis and RIEs. To sustain gains, leaders are looking to create true "protected time" for staff to engage in MyCare activities. They also want to launch a formal reward and recognition program to further encourage involvement in MyCare.

The Journey So Far

Tan Tock Seng Hospital is an organization with a strong foundation in performance improvement principles and activities. Despite financial stability and high-quality indicators at the hospital, leaders chose to adopt the Lean approach to improve efficiency and maximize use of existing space. They created MyCare, a program tailored for Lean implementation at TTSH, and utilized Lean tools to improve processes across the entire hospital. Focus on areas like discharge and patient flow through short stay units yielded increased capacity and enhanced care, By implementing Lean simultaneously on units with similar flow characteristics, hospital leaders achieved rapid improvement in efficiency. By implementing Lean, TTSH leaders were able to bring the organization to an even higher level of performance in quality and efficiency than before.

The X Factor at Tan Tock Seng Hospital: A Pervasive Culture of Improvement

The pre-existing organizational culture at TTSH was an essential element in the successful implementation of Lean at the hospital. Cultivated over years of involvement in performance improvement initiatives, the TTSH culture was highly influenced by the culture of its umbrella organization, the integrated health system National Healthcare Group (NHG). Leaders of NHG set the expectation that all member organizations would be committed to patient-centric performance improvement. "Patients First"—the articulated philosophy of the system—emphasizes the importance of designing and providing care "around our patients' needs, not the other way around." Upon this foundation, TTSH leaders built a culture of improvement that pervades the organization and was highly conducive to success with Lean.

Years of dedicated effort in "bottom-up" initiatives had created a high level of competency and knowledge around process improvement. When organizational leaders launched the hospital's Lean-based program MyCare, which emphasizes the responsibility of each employee for quality improvement and patient safety, it proved a fertile ground for explosive growth and rapid improvement.

Since the chapter was written, Professor Choo has been elevated to the position of CEO of Tan Tok Seng. Under the professor's leadership, TTSH is taking the use of Lean to new heights, including using Lean Design to create the architectural specification for the new three-hundred-and-fifty-plus-bed National Centre for Disease Control in Singapore, a joint TTSH and Ministry of Health project.

About the Author

Marc S. Hafer

Marc Hafer learned the Toyota Production System and Lean tools working with one of the foremost US practitioners, the Shingijutsu Consulting Group. His experience in Lean transformation ranges from manufacturing companies that produce high-volume, standard products to entrepreneurial organizations creating lower-volume, custom-engineered products. He has successfully applied Lean principles throughout entire enterprises, from shop floor manufacturing to office administrative/engineering functions and field construction crews.

When Marc Hafer joined Simpler® in 2002, he brought years of leadership experience in sales, marketing, product development, strategic planning, and general management with him. His skills as a gifted teacher and visionary leader were evident from the beginning, and he quickly rose through the ranks, eventually becoming president of Simpler North America in 2007 and CEO of Simpler Holdings in 2009.

Today, he is responsible for overseeing the strategic direction of Simpler Consulting around the world. Marc also coaches client leadership teams. He is a frequent speaker at industry conferences and volunteers in support of industry organizations such as the Association for Manufacturing Excellence, the Shingo Prize, the Joint Commission on Accreditation of Healthcare Organizations and the Institute for Healthcare Improvement.

6311973R00059

Made in the USA
San Bernardino, CA
05 December 2013